D1516581

WITHDRAWN

THE BARBARIC COUNTER-REVOLUTION

The Barbaric
Counter-Revolution

Cause and Cure by W. W. Rostow

 University of Texas Press, Austin

Requests for permission to reproduce material from
this work should be sent to Permissions, University
of Texas Press, Box 7819, Austin, Texas 78712.

LIBRARY OF CONGRESS CATALOGING IN PUBLICATION DATA
Rostow, W. W. (Walt Whitman), 1916–
    The barbaric counter-revolution.
    1. United States—Economic policy—1981–
2. United States—Economic policy—1971–1981.
I. Title.
HC106.8.R675   1983   338.973   83-6638
ISBN 0-292-70749-5

For Elspeth

Contents

CHARTS

Preface

At 3:00 on the morning of December 15, 1982, when sleep was light, I got up and outlined this book in just about the form that it now appears. It responds to a deepening concern with the cumulative human, national, and international damage done by the economic policies pursued by the United States over the past four years—a concern that by no means ended with the coming of an economic revival in early 1983.

This book is evidently a tract for the times, a fact reflected in its lack of footnotes and the other paraphernalia of academic writing. But it is rooted in my work over the past decade on the history, problems, and prospects of the world economy incorporated in *How It All Began, The World Economy: History and Prospect, Getting from Here to There,* and *Why the Poor Get Richer and the Rich Slow Down.*

It reflects also a quite different enterprise. I have been writing a series of short books around the theme Ideas and Action. The books focus retrospectively on the role of abstract concepts in specific key decisions along with all the other more mundane forces in play; they attempt to trace out the consequences of the decision and reflect on both the substance of the decision and the process which led to it.

Although this book looks forward as well as backward, it belongs with the Ideas and Action Series. One of its central themes is that the macroeconomic concepts of mainstream economics, Keynesian and monetarist—generated in the 1930s, elaborated and applied from 1945 to 1972—are grossly inadequate for the world that emerged in the 1970s and for the foreseeable problems of the 1980s and 1990s. We are, in a sense, repeating the tragedy of the interwar years. Then economists and the politicians who depended on them were so imprisoned by the concepts and policies that worked before 1914 that they could not understand or come to grips with the problems that emerged after 1920. By the time they began to get a handle on economic affairs, the world economy was irretrievably fragmented, the Japanese military and Hitler were in power. The time lag in the minds and concepts of economists and in the public policies which flowed from them must be reckoned among the causes of the Second World War.

There is no need for history to repeat itself; and, of course, it never repeats exactly. Nevertheless, what happened between 1920 and 1939 should remind us of the possible cost of applying ideas from the past to situations where they do not adequately apply. Several readers of the book in draft noted that the use of the word "barbaric" in the title might appear to impugn the motives of those who have conducted the counter-revolution with which it deals. There is, of course, no such attack on the motives of those with whom I disagree in the text. Nevertheless, I gave the matter considerable thought. I concluded that the title is just. In the long sweep of history, barbaric results have often flowed from the actions of men seeking goals they judged to be good.

I am indebted to a number of colleagues, in Austin and elsewhere, who generously helped as critics and in mobilizing data and judgments on the evolution of the economy in recent years, notably, Victor Arnold, Francis Bator, Elizabeth Bossong, William Fisher, James Galbraith, John Kenneth Galbraith, Daniel Garnick, David Kendrick, Michael Kennedy, George Kozmetsky, Leonard H. Marks, Ray Marshall, George Perry, Felix Rohatyn, and Susan Walter. Pedro Fraile helped me exploit the facilities of Project Mulhall, the computerized economic history data base at the University of Texas at Austin, to generate the materials for most of the charts.

I should acknowledge another debt. In my last meeting with Sir Michael Postan before his death in December 1981, he raised with me the likelihood of substantial chronic unemployment. He judged that the new technologies being diffused throughout the advanced industrial world, combined with the erosion of the old basic industries, would render a large number of unskilled and semiskilled workers unemployable. Respecting his insight, as I had for more than forty years, I set about trying to test his hypothesis as it might apply to the American economy. From that exercise emerged the broad argument outlined in chapter 5 which sets the framework for the more detailed prescriptions of chapter 6.

I wish to thank, once again, Frances Knape, who typed the manuscript, and Lois Nivens, who, as so many times in the past, helped as sharp-eyed editor, spotter of relevant materials, and in many other indispensable ways.

I wish, finally, to thank my wife, Elspeth Davies Rostow, to whom this book is dedicated. For quite a long time now she has, at every time of decision, urged me to go forward, to set down such insights as my work has generated, and then supported my efforts in every way, including, as in this case, the role of acute but constructive critic.

APRIL 1983   W. W. ROSTOW
AUSTIN, TEXAS

THE BARBARIC COUNTER-REVOLUTION

1. The Central Theme

The advanced industrial countries of the Western world are in the grip of a barbaric counter-revolution. It is eroding the physical and social infrastructure of Western societies, endangering their alliances, driving the developing regions into a potentially explosive phase of stagnation, and threatening the precarious equilibrium of a fragile, divided global community in a thermonuclear age.

This short book is an effort to help break out of that counter-revolution and to generate civilized policies for the 1980s and beyond.

The counter-revolution is endemic in the industrialized North. It is being conducted in some countries reluctantly and defensively. In Great Britain it has been pursued with conviction and verve since the accession to power of Mrs. Thatcher's Conservative government in May 1979. Its center, however, is in the United States. There the counter-revolution can be dated arbitrarily from the imposition of a restrictive money-supply policy by the Federal Reserve on October 6, 1979, and an unprecedented rise in real interest rates. The counter-revolution widened and gained clarity and momentum with the coming to responsibility of Mr. Reagan in January 1981.

The world economy cannot break out of its grip until American policy is radically altered. Through a natural and inevitable process, the proportion of output of the United States relative to the global total has greatly declined since the end of the Second World War; but, as of 1979, it was still about 21 percent. The equivalent rough figure for Great Britain was 4 percent; France 5 percent; West Germany 7 percent; Japan 9 percent; the U.S.S.R. 12 percent. The influence of American policy is even greater than these relative figures would suggest. American interest rates, for example, have global consequences, given the still powerful role of American capital markets and the dollar in the world's financial system.

The diffusion of economic power, which has been going on for about thirty-five years, will, no doubt, proceed. But the United States government and the American people still bear an inescapable responsibility in the world economy. Therefore, this book will focus primarily on American policy.

American policy in recent years can be authentically described as barbaric because it has resulted in an irretrievable loss of real output in the United States of about $750 billion during the three-year period 1980–1982. It has yielded unemployment rates averaging over 8 percent for this period, reaching almost 11 percent in December 1982, with all the attendant human frustration and tragedy those figures imply. It has widened the previously narrowing gap between white and nonwhite incomes and is generating a large, corrosive social problem, with nonwhite teenage unemployment running at about 40 percent. It has raised the level of bankruptcies to heights not experienced since the worst of the 1930s. It has cut capacity utilization in manufacturing to less than 70 percent, throttled industrial investment, rendering impossible the revitalization of old basic industries and the full exploitation of new technologies in those industries. It has damped the momentum of the dynamic high-technology sectors, on which the place of the United States in the world economy will increasingly depend. It has generated extraordinary federal deficits, for about two-thirds of those deficits is due to the recession. It has driven federal, state, and local governments to permit basic services to degenerate: roads, highways, and bridges; water supply and sewage disposal; police and fire protection; schools, libraries, and museums. It has endangered the social security system. It has been accompanied by a thrust at the federal level to reduce social outlays, which, indeed, deserve a careful pruning out and proportioning to the real growth rate but not the rather indiscriminate surgery now being attempted. It has rendered the national and international financial structure fragile and vulnerable to a crisis which could plunge the world economy into a deep depression.

It will require extraordinarily perverse skill to prevent some kind of recovery in 1983. By all conventional estimates, the American economy will be running with not much less than 10 percent unemployment and not much more than 70 percent capacity utilization at the close of the year. The initial surge could be stronger than the conventional estimates suggest if the world oil price continues to subside for a while, but the expansion will be without a secure foundation and subject to early reversal.

This dismal prospect exists because the years of recession since 1979—with all their economic, social, and human costs—have provided no method for assuring that a robust, sustained revival would not yield a rise in interest rates, accelerated inflation, acute balance of payments pressures, and, before long, another recession.

The blunt fact is that the Reagan administration has no other plan to avoid a rising inflation rate than to maintain a kind of Marxist reserve army of the unemployed. And the Democrats have offered no authentic alternative that would reconcile rapid, sustained growth with control over inflation.

This is a truly barbaric performance for a rich, well-educated, technologically resourceful, democratic society. It is the central theme of this book that our present plight is unnecessary.

But counter-revolutions happen because revolutions fail. And this is the case in the United States and most of the advanced industrial world. The revolution that failed was the particular pattern of intellectual concepts, public policy, and institutional behavior generated in the historically unique, sustained boom of the 1950s and 1960s that ended with the explosion of grain prices at the end of 1972 and the quadrupling of oil prices in 1973–1974. The revolution failed, like others, because it did not adjust to the reality of new, unpredicted circumstances. After stumbling through the sharp recession of 1974–1975, the world economy experienced a phase of infirm recovery to be struck again by the second oil price jump of 1979–1980. And the counter-revolution began in earnest. It is necessary, therefore, to account for the prior revolution, the counter-revolution that followed, and then to prescribe remedy. That is what this book attempts to do.

2. How We Got Here: 1951–1981

The place to begin is with the unique expansion of the world economy in the 1950s and 1960s. It is well dramatized in table 1. The average 3.8 percent rate of real growth per capita in the advanced industrial countries was more than three times the average for the previous 130 years.

The boom was shared by the developing countries. In the 1960s they grew at an average rate of over 5.6 percent, a higher rate than for the industrialized countries (4.9 percent). Average per capita growth was lower in the developing regions because of higher rates of population increase, but they outpaced the pre-1914 per capita growth rates of the presently advanced industrial countries.

The world economy as a whole experienced growth in industrial production during the 1950s and 1960s of 5.6 percent, in world trade of about 7.3 percent, exceeding by a substantial margin any prior performance.

Growth was also much steadier than it had been over the previous two centuries. Cyclical fluctuations did not disappear from the scene, but for a quarter-century unemployment virtually ceased to be a problem in Western Europe and Japan. And in the slower-growing, more volatile United States, unemployment averaged over this period just about the level of the prosperous 1920s.

As table 1 indicates, the rates of real growth in the industrial countries in 1950–1973, while in all cases unique, were by no means uniform. Japan headed the league in growth, followed by Germany, Austria, Italy, Finland, Belgium, and the Netherlands, all of which had felt directly the impact of the Second World War. The United States is at the bottom of the

TABLE 1. Growth of Output (GDP at Constant Prices) per Head of Population, 1700–1979 (Annual Average Compound Growth Rates)

Country	1700–1820	1820–70	1870–1913	1913–50	1950–73	1973–79	1820–1979
Australia		n.a.	0.6	0.7	2.5	1.3	n.a.
Austria		0.7	1.5	0.2	5.0	3.1	1.5
Belgium		1.9	1.0	0.7	3.6	2.1	1.7
Canada		n.a.	2.0	1.3	3.0	2.1	n.a.
Denmark		0.9	1.6	1.5	3.3	1.8	1.6
Finland		n.a.	1.7	1.7	4.2	2.0	n.a.
France	0.3[a]	1.0	1.5	1.0	4.1	2.6	1.6
Germany		1.1	1.6	0.7	5.0	2.6	1.8
Italy		n.a.	0.8	0.7	4.8	2.0	n.a.
Japan		0.0	1.5	0.5	8.4	3.0	1.8
Netherlands	−0.1	1.5	0.9	1.1	3.5	1.7	1.5
Norway		1.0	1.3	2.1	3.1	3.9	1.8
Sweden		0.6	2.1	2.2	3.1	1.5	1.8
Switzerland		1.7	1.2	1.5	3.1	−0.2	1.6
U.K.	0.4	1.5	1.0	0.9	2.5	1.3	1.4
U.S.A.		1.4	2.0	1.6	2.2	1.9	1.8
Arithmetic average	0.2	1.1	1.4	1.2	3.8	2.0	1.6

[a]1701/10–1820.

SOURCE: Angus Maddison, "Capitalist Economic Performance since 1820," in L. Jörberg and N. Rosenberg, eds., *Technical Change, Employment and Investment* (Lund: Department of Economic History, University of Lund, 1982), p. 155.

list. We shall consider later the factors that appear to have determined the shape of this array. Here it is sufficient to note that those toward the bottom of the list, with lower rates of investment and productivity increase, tended to experience chronic pressure on their balance of payments. The United States, for example, began to lose gold systematically, starting in 1958.

The remarkable rise in the real incomes of families over this period brought about a true economic and social revolution in Western Europe, Japan, and the United States. A way of life, already familiar in the United States and Canada, spread out over Western Europe and Japan: the mass ownership of the automobile, an increasingly standard package of durable goods and migration to suburbia, rates of increase in enrollments in higher education twice or more than twice the rates of increase in real income, similar disproportionate increases in outlays for medical care. There was, in fact, a general tendency for consumers to receive a higher proportion of their total consumption in the form of increased government benefits: old-age pensions, health insurance, unemployment benefits, and other welfare allowances. Transfer payments of this kind rose, for a sample of advanced industrial countries, from 9.3 percent of GDP in 1950 to 20.6 percent in 1977. For the United States the figures were lower: 7.9 percent to 15.4 percent. Even with the high real growth rates of the period, this was, evidently, a process which could not proceed indefinitely.

The new affluence permitted European workers to drive their families south for vacations on the Mediterranean; Americans to visit national parks and to travel abroad in unexampled numbers; and the Japanese, for the first time in history, to go touring in Europe and the United States. All this, like any successful revolution, created problems. Levels of pollution rose in the Mediterranean; the National Park Service was hard-pressed to maintain the common treasures entrusted to its care; starting in 1962 with Rachel Carson's *Silent Spring* and building up to the Club of Rome's *Limits to Growth* in 1970, acute anxiety developed as to whether the earth could cope with the rates of growth in population and output under way; the new scale of higher education, not always matched by adequate facilities, reduced its elite character and prerogatives, stirring unrest among some of the students; and, in a pattern described at least as far back as Plato's *Republic*, a margin of the affluent young in many countries, taking the new state of affairs for granted, reacted against its flaws and sought new, more personal, and less materialistic objectives for themselves and their societies.

Nevertheless, since modern economic growth began in Britain in the 1780s, there had never been an equivalent protracted phase of economic and social progress measured by standards most men and women would accept as valid. And, perhaps because the easiest of all human transitions is to move up in the world, growth at the high rates of these two decades came pretty much to be taken for granted. Citizens and organized groups, such as labor unions, sought to assure that they received a goodly share of the expanding pie. There were, as always, strands of simple greed in all of this, but also a creditable noblesse oblige among the electorates of the advanced industrial democracies—that is, a willingness to see part of the increment in real income tapped off to assist the less advantaged, both at home and in the developing regions.

As the boom came to be recognized as a rather remarkable phenomenon, a number of scholars set about analyzing its causes. Their books emphasized a variety of forces at work, for example, the rebuilding and modernization of economies damaged by war after a prior period of protracted depression, the bringing into industry in Western Europe of reserve supplies of labor from agriculture or abroad, the rapid absorption in Western Europe and Japan of hitherto unapplied technologies, maintenance by governments of high levels of effective demand.

Not many citizens or politicians or, indeed, economists read the learned detailed studies of the anatomy of the boom. If there was an intellectual consensus, it was that the Keynesian doctrines, generated out of the Great Depression of the 1930s, linked to the capacity to measure accurately the components of national income, had put democratic societies in operational command of their economic destinies. We could now, it came to be believed, manipulate the components of the aggregate level of effective demand through fiscal and monetary policy in ways which permitted us to enjoy relatively steady full employment and rapid growth, with modest rates of inflation. Theories of effective demand which asserted this proposition were refined, simplified, and taught confidently to undergraduates in macroeconomic courses throughout the advanced industrial world. The doctrine came to be accepted by politicians of all parties, an outcome climaxed by Richard Nixon's reported proclamation, on January 4, 1971, "I am now a Keynesian in economics."

This period was, of course, not without its economic and political debates. The monetarists argued that Keynesian devices (that is, tax and expenditure policy) were ineffective and often mistimed and misdirected. They counseled that the line between high growth and inflation should be held by a steady, stubborn, publicly announced rate of increase in the money supply geared to the real, noninflationary rate of growth the economy was capable of sustaining (that is, the rate of growth of the working force plus the average rate of growth of productivity per worker). Others argued, as they had since the early days of the New Deal, that the rate of growth of government authority in general and of public expenditures in particular was excessive and would lead to a fatal weakening of the private sector and the erosion of personal freedom in democratic societies.

A few, including, notably, President Kennedy, judged that fiscal and monetary policies were insufficient to control inflation, that supplementary understandings among business, labor, and government were required to gear the average rate of increase of money wages to the average rate of productivity increase, and that public policy should seek an acceleration in productivity. Given the pressures on the U.S. balance of payments he inherited, these were not matters of abstract theory. Indeed, Kennedy restrained his Keynesian advisers and refused to request a tax cut from the Congress until he had achieved a working approximation of equality between money wage and productivity increases.

Nevertheless, as passages of history go, the period 1950–1972 was, so far as the advanced industrial countries are concerned, one of confidence—even complacency—based on the generally unexamined assumption that the uniquely high rates of growth that had emerged from reconstruction after the Second World War were to be regarded essentially as normal and that they would persist if intelligent fiscal and monetary policies were followed.

For our purposes, the central fact about this period is that neither the mainstream economists (monetarist as well as Keynesian) nor the political leaders who relied upon them understood why the great boom had occurred and why, in the form it assumed, it was inherently transient.

The boom occurred primarily because of an accidental convergence of two factors, neither of which has a place in conventional macroeconomics, with its virtually exclusive concern with the level of total effective demand. First, a dramatic decline in the prices of basic commodities (food, raw materials, and energy) relative to those of manufactures (see chart 1B).

CHART 1. Relative Prices, 1951–1982

A. Crude Materials and Finished Goods Prices

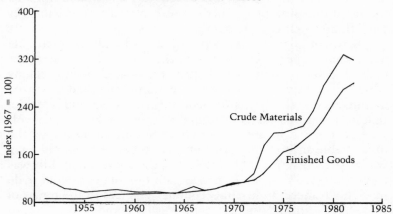

B. Ratio of Crude Materials to Finished Goods Prices

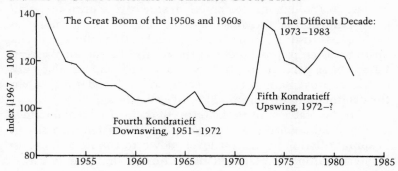

NOTE: For an explanation of Kondratieff cycles, see chapter 5.
SOURCE: *Economic Report of the President to the Congress, February 1983*, pp. 227–228.

Second, the existence of a large backlog of technology which had not yet been applied in Western Europe and Japan. A third factor at work throughout the advanced industrial world was the rapid diffusion of synthetic fibers, plastics, television, jet aircraft, and a range of lesser innovations.

Between 1938 and 1951 prices of food and raw materials had risen 257 percent in world markets, fuel 140 percent, but manufactures by only 106 percent. For countries and regions which primarily imported basic commodities and exported manufactures, the terms of trade turned grossly unfavorable; that is, it required a larger volume of exports to buy a given volume of imports. In the case of Great Britain, for example, the unfavorable shift in the terms of trade between 1938 and 1951 was 24 percent. For the United States, the unfavorable shift was 32 percent (see chart 2). Depending on the role of foreign trade in each advanced, industrial economy, changes in the terms of trade have a strong, direct effect on real income.

After 1951, relative prices and the terms of trade sharply reversed. Food and raw materials prices declined at a decelerating rate to a trough in 1964 and then slowly rose until the grain price explosion at the close of 1972. The prices of manufactured goods rose slowly after 1953, accelerating after 1970. The upshot was an improvement in the terms of trade for Western Europe of 24 percent, for the U.S. of about 22 percent. The bulk of the improvement occurred between 1951 and 1964, when the decline in basic commodity prices bottomed out.

The favorable shift in the terms of trade lifted real incomes in industrial countries and regions, and it assisted mightily in keeping inflation at modest levels down to the mid 1960s. In Western Europe and Japan it had a further dramatic effect. It brought real family incomes up to a level where an increasing proportion of the population could afford an automobile and durable consumer goods. In France, for example, the proportion of households equipped with refrigerators rose from 7.5 percent in 1954 to 52 percent in 1964; in Britain, from 7 percent in 1954 to 40 percent in 1966. There was less scope for the durable consumer boom in the United States. By 1957, 96 percent of American households were equipped with refrigerators, and 75 percent owned automobiles. Only freezers, driers, and air con-

CHART 2. U.S. Terms of Trade (Export Divided by Import Prices), 1933–1982

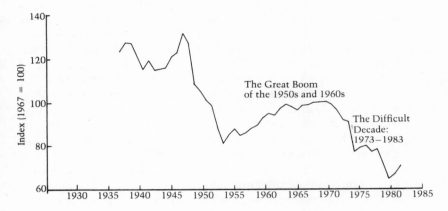

SOURCE: International Monetary Fund and Department of Commerce.

ditioners remained still to be installed in 70 percent of American homes by 1967.

The fundamental point here is that Western Europe and Japan, because of their lag behind the United States in automobiles and durable consumer goods, rapidly developed a new industrial structure, incorporating technologies hitherto more fully exploited in the United States. The exploitation of this technological backlog substantially explains the higher growth rates in Western Europe and Japan than in the United States.

In addition, as noted earlier, the whole advanced industrial world moved with great élan into television, synthetic fibers, and plastics.

These technological possibilities, converging with the lift in real incomes provided by favorable terms of trade, essentially explain the great boom of the 1950s and 1960s.

Surely, macroeconomic policy played a role. But, on the whole, the macroeconomists in governments were dealing with economies driven forward by powerful twin engines they did not fully understand, and they tended to mistake their marginal guidance of the economy for the basic motive forces at work. In fact, probably the most important role of purposeful fiscal and monetary policies in this period, for most advanced industrial countries (the U.S. in the early 1960s was something of an exception), was to restrain excessive expansions when they created balance of payments pressures or dangerous inflationary tendencies. And, as was generally understood, one of the most important positive macroforces was automatic—that is, the effect on recessions or potential recessions of unemployment benefits and other welfare outlays mandated by law that increased despite the fall in tax revenues the recession brought about. Thus, a cushioning Keynesian increase in the governmental deficits emerged promptly when recessions occurred.

In the late 1960s, forces came into play which undermined the foundations of the great boom:

— As noted earlier, basic commodity prices began to rise after 1964, removing an important damper on inflation.

— Specifically, the proportion of world grain reserves (including idle arable land) to consumption declined from ninety-five days of annual grain consumption in 1961 to fifty-one days in 1971—a decline exacerbated by the poor Indian harvests of 1965–1967. Reserves were sufficient to hold the wheat price steady, but the prices of rice and soybeans began gradually to rise. With attenuating stocks, the world's grain supply system became vulnerable to the convergence of bad harvests in several parts of the world which occurred in 1972.

— Similarly with respect to energy, the price of oil, falling relative to the price level in the 1950s and 1960s, along with the powerful increase in demand brought about by the great boom, led to extremely rapid increases in energy consumption. World consumption of energy increased at an annual average rate of 5.6 percent in the 1960s, as the diffusion of the automobile and durable consumer goods proceeded, as well as the rapid expansion of energy-intensive industries such as petrochemicals. Meanwhile, the advanced industrial countries progressively shifted toward the use of oil and natural gas at the expense of coal; and the U.S., a net energy exporter in 1950, came to import about 10 percent of its energy consumption by 1972. U.S. petroleum production peaked out in 1970; natural gas production leveled off in 1971–1973 and began to decline. OPEC, in existence since 1960, perceived promptly that monopoly powers were within its grasp if it could maintain inner discipline. And in 1973 it acted on that perception.

— Meanwhile, the technological basis for the great boom began to erode from about the mid 1960s. In a quite normal process, the rapid growth sectors of the 1950s and early 1960s decelerated—for example, motor vehicles, plastics, and synthetic fibers. For reasons operating on the side both of supply (a gradual slowing down of technological change) and of demand (the limits of the market), deceleration is the normal time path for a sector incorporating a new technology. The expansion of certain service sectors (for example, health services, education, travel) continued, and a new phase in electronics and computers began to emerge. Nevertheless, the average rate of productivity increase and the rise in real wages in the advanced industrial countries began to decline. For example, the productivity of investment in eight advanced industrial countries (measured by what economists call the marginal capital–output ratio) fell by 19 percent between 1965 and 1970. In the United States, the rate of increase of output per person employed in the nonfarm business sector, which averaged 3.3 percent in 1961–1965, fell to 1.5 percent in 1966–1970, a decline exacerbated by the recession of 1969–1970 but evident in the average for the first three prosperous years of the period (2.6 percent) (see chart 3B). This retardation in productivity converged with the rising tendency in basic commodity prices to lift inflation rates and to slow down sharply the rate of increase in real wages.

The conventional wisdom among mainstream economists is to attribute the emergence of somewhat higher inflation rates in the second half of the 1960s to enlarged U.S. expenditures for the war in Southeast Asia and the delay, until 1968, in bringing about a compensatory rise in federal tax rates. There is, almost certainly, an element of truth in this proposition.

The rise in military expenditures as a proportion of GNP was real but modest in these years: 7.7 percent in 1964; 7.1 percent in 1965; 8 percent in 1966; 8.9 percent in 1967; 8.1 percent in 1969 (see chart 4). There was, in fact, some absolute decline in 1969. Nevertheless, the average unemployment level was under 4 percent over the period 1966–1969 and capacity utilization was high, although it declined from a peak in 1966.

CHART 3. The Core Inflation Rate (Nonfarm Business Sector),
1951–1982

A. Rate of Change of Compensation per Hour

B. Rate of Change in Output per Hour

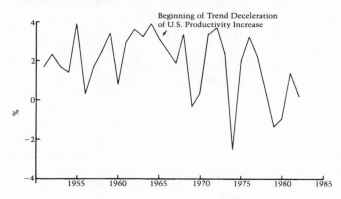

C. Rate of Change in Unit Labor Cost

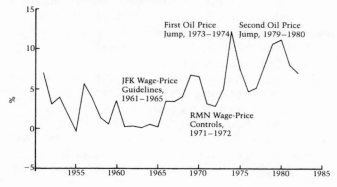

SOURCE: *Economic Report of the President to the Congress, February 1983*,
p. 209.

There was, also, a minirecession in 1967 as the Federal Reserve raised interest rates in the face of congressional unwillingness to raise taxes. But, no doubt, a tax increase in 1966 rather than 1968 would have been marginally helpful.

On the other hand, the reversal of the trend in world basic commodity prices from the trough in 1964 and the deceleration of productivity evidently played an important role in raising inflation rates. The former led to demands for larger money wage increases; the latter led to a further rise in unit labor costs, the most basic measure of the inflation rate, for unit labor costs are measured roughly by subtracting the average increase in productivity from the average increase in money wages. More than a third of the increase in unit labor costs for the period 1966–1969 over their level of 1961–1965 is due to the deceleration in productivity as opposed to higher money wages; and the rise in money wages is the product not merely of tight labor markets but also of an effort to compensate for the pressure on the cost of living of the rise in basic commodity prices after 1964.

CHART 4. Defense Outlays as Percent of GNP, 1950–1987 (Projected)

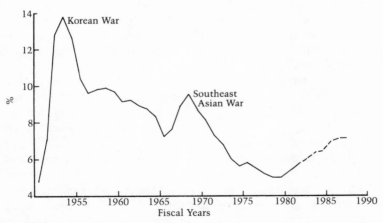

SOURCE: *Economic Report of the President to the Congress, February 1982,* p. 85.

In short, when grain prices rose 50 percent in 1972–1974 and the international oil price quadrupled in 1973–1974 (yielding an 83 percent rise in U.S. domestic fuel prices), the twin foundations of the great boom were already eroding. And these events, in effect, definitively turned off the process of rapid growth which the United States, Western Europe, and Japan had enjoyed for a generation. The terms of trade shifted radically against the advanced industrial countries. For the United States, the deterioration was about 20 percent by 1974, despite a large increase in high-priced grain exports.

The mechanism at work in the various industrialized countries was similar, although its net impact varied:

— Real wages declined or decelerated under the impact of the adverse shift in the terms of trade.

— Acute balance of payments pressures stemming from the oil price increase led to policies of fiscal and monetary restraint (including high interest rates) as well as to more direct energy conservation measures.

— The rise in energy prices, reduced levels of employment, and real income and high interest rates led, in particular, to a decline in postponable consumption expenditures (notably on automobiles, durable consumer goods, and housing), as well as to reduced consumption outlays in general, a decline that was promptly transmitted to levels of investment.

— Wage-push (or unit cost) inflation (see chart 3C) accelerated, as those unions with bargaining leverage sought to compensate for reduced real wages by demanding higher money wage increases.

— Efforts of varying success were made to expand exports to the oil-rich nations and others, but these were inhibited in the short run by the limited absorptive capacity of some of the major oil producers and by the endemic world recession which gathered momentum in 1974.

— Business expectations, particularly optimistic in the boom of 1972–1973, shifted toward caution or pessimism, exacerbating the decline in investment induced by high interest rates and reduced consumption outlays, while compensatory investment in alternative energy resources and conservation expanded only slowly.

— Similarly, the dour expectations of private consumers, in

an environment of both accelerated inflation and rising unemployment, led to a rise in savings.

Through this complex convergence of forces, the real losses in output suffered in 1974 by the advanced industrial nations were about twice the amount transferred to the oil producers due to the fourfold increase in their export prices.

The traumatic experience of 1973–1975 demonstrated that inflation could be a much more complex matter than it appeared in macroeconomic textbooks. There the focus was exclusively on demand-pull inflation, that is, on a level of overall demand for labor, goods, and services so high that it bid up money wages in tight labor markets and bid up prices in sectors where limitations of capacity yielded bottlenecks. In 1975 the consumer price index rose 9 percent, unemployment was up to 8.5 percent, and capacity utilization was down to 73 percent. Unemployment was higher, capacity utilization lower, than in any year since the Great Depression of the 1930s. This was, indeed, stagflation.

There are, in fact, three kinds of inflation: demand-pull, raw materials-push, and wage-push. The United States, as a continental economy, has not experienced demand-pull inflation since the 1960s. The 1972–1974 explosion of agricultural and energy prices is a clear example of raw materials-push inflation. Wage-push inflation exists when the average rate of money wage increases exceeds the average rate of productivity increases. Unit costs rise. This is often called the basic or core inflation rate because some 70 percent of all costs in the American economy are labor costs. No policy to control inflation can succeed unless core inflation is held, essentially, at zero for the long pull.

But raw materials-push and wage-push inflation are not independent phenomena. As noted earlier, when the cost of living rose sharply in 1973–1975, money wage increases were demanded and granted in a fruitless effort to shield real wages, which declined by over 7 percent (see chart 3A). But the rise in money wages accelerated the rise in prices like the second-stage booster of a rocket. The rise in unit labor costs was compounded by a sharp decline in productivity in 1974.

The world oil price leveled off after its initial quadrupling; the real price of oil, therefore, fell in a generally inflationary environment; good harvests eased the pressure on food prices; and the world economy recovered to a degree over the period 1975–1979. The inflation rate declined, but the wage-push element of inflation continued at a higher level than earlier. Unit labor costs, damped by President Nixon's wage and price controls, had increased at an average rate of only 4.2 percent in 1970–1972, 6.3 percent in 1976–1978. Recovery thus took place with a higher plateau of core inflation.

Then came the second oil price jump of 1978–1979, triggered by the Iranian Revolution and the cutback of Iranian oil production and exports. The 1974–1975 convulsive rise in the inflation rate, with money wage increases and a decline in productivity providing a second-stage booster, was repeated in 1979–1980; but the decline in productivity was markedly more severe, reflecting the now protracted prior period of low investment.

The economy began to revive slowly after August 1980, as real oil prices again declined and monetary restraint was eased, perhaps with an eye on the forthcoming presidential elections. The inflation rate, however, continued at double-digit levels and interest rates remained high. Unemployment stood at 7.6 percent in October 1980. This was not a wholesome setting in which to face a general election.

So much for the bare facts.

Now what did the Nixon, Ford, and Carter administrations do when confronted by the new international economic environment? To paraphrase the Abbé Sieyès on his life during the French Revolution, they tried to survive. None developed coherent and effective policies for dealing with the interlocked energy, balance of payments, inflation, unemployment, and productivity problems that emerged. Mainly, they tried to use the familiar tools of fiscal and monetary policy to deal with circumstances in which they were clearly insufficient.

Nevertheless, a few initiatives should be noted.

First, the Nixon administration strongly, the Carter administration weakly, sought to get at the core inflation rate by restraining wages and prices. The Nixon experiment came in 1971–1972, before the explosive increases in grain and oil prices of 1972–1974. A weakening of the American balance of payments in the second quarter of 1971 posed a harsh choice

for the administration in the summer of that year: either induce a recession, which would cut back imports and relieve
pressure on an overvalued dollar still locked into the Bretton
Woods system with its tie between the dollar and gold, or break
the Bretton Woods linkage and impose price and wage controls.
The latter option was made possible by a 1970 amendment to
the Defense Production Act of 1950, granting the president
such powers. Although Nixon opposed the amendment, he
used it vigorously in the balance of payments crisis of the summer of 1971. The sequence of controls initiated in August
yielded over the next sixteen months a sharp rise in capacity
utilization and productivity (3.7 percent), virtually no rise in
the rate of increase of money wages, a decline in unit labor
costs to 2.8 percent, a decline in interest rates, a decline in the
rate of increase in consumer prices to 3.2 percent, and a rise
in average real weekly earnings of 4.1 percent. The explosion
of grain and oil prices in 1973–1974 is often linked to the
Nixon phase of wage-price controls, as if it represented a break-
away from unnatural constraint in 1971–1972. This is not the
case. As noted earlier, the explosions occurred because of long-
generating tensions in grain and oil markets triggered by the
failed harvests of 1972–1973 and OPEC's perception, in 1973,
that the cartel at last had the leverage to quadruple prices.

Just as analyses of the rise in the inflation rate after 1964
appear to be affected by the passions stirred by the war in Viet-
nam, analyses of the 1971–1972 experience with wage and
price controls seem to be colored by political biases. So-called
liberals find it difficult to credit Nixon with a useful response
to an authentic crisis. So-called conservatives, many of whom
opposed Nixon's policies at the time, are, in retrospect, extremely critical of the episode. Indeed, Nixon's memoirs reflect this attitude. The fact is, however, that it yielded, in the
short run, a benign result and created for Nixon a favorable domestic economic setting for the 1972 presidential election, as
it was no doubt designed to do.

Although it deserves more careful and objective analysis
than it has been granted, this brief adventure was flawed in several respects.

The basic flaw in Nixon's policy was that it was announced
as temporary. It did not end inflationary expectations. Business

and labor jockeyed for position in anticipation (correctly) of the lifting of controls after the 1972 election. Nixon's policy was a tactical device, not a strategy, for dealing with inflation. In addition, by including energy prices within the control system, the policy helped complicate the design of energy policy later in the decade. As I shall later argue (chapter 6), the Nixon policy of 1971–1972 is not an appropriate model for a long-run approach to inflation control, although elements in that policy might prove useful.

As accelerating inflation reasserted itself in the post-1975 recovery, the Carter administration also sought to act directly on the inflation rate in the last three years of its responsibility. The Council on Wage and Price Stability (CWPS) was set up in 1978. Its membership included representatives of business and labor. The 1970 sanction for presidential control over prices and wages had lapsed, and its reinstallation was not sought by Carter from the Congress. The CWPS aimed gradually to damp wage and price increases by formulating standards and seeking voluntary compliance. The Carter administration claimed some positive results; but, clearly, the strategy was, at best, only marginally effective.

Carter also laid before the Congress a tax-based incomes policy (TIP) which would provide tangible incentives to firms and workers to slow the rate of inflation. Firms and workers that complied with publicly enunciated price and wage standards would be rewarded with tax credits. There were also versions of such proposals where those not in compliance could face tax penalties. The TIP concept was not subjected to much public discussion or acted upon by the Congress.

In the summer of 1979 the Carter administration, like the Nixon administration eight years earlier, confronted a major international financial crisis. The second oil price increase, against the background of accelerating American inflation, weakened the U.S. balance of payments and the dollar, which remained a key currency despite the demise of the Bretton Woods system in December 1971. The dollar had fallen 18 percent relative to all other currencies between March 1977 and September 1979, 33 percent against the German mark. Amidst fears for the viability of the international financial system, as funds shifted away from the dollar to stronger currencies, Carter was pressed hard by the leaders of the other advanced industrial countries—notably at the Tokyo summit meeting of June 1979—to bring the U.S. balance of payments and inflation under control and thus to restore confidence in the dollar. Unlike Nixon in 1971, he chose to do this by an orthodox policy of monetary restraint and high interest rates. The prime interest rate rose from 11½ percent in July 1979 to 19½ percent in April 1980. The dollar and the balance of payments did, indeed, strengthen to a degree as a result of the consequent sharp recession and the beginning of a decline in the real oil price.

As noted earlier, it was in October 1979 that the Carter administration acquiesced in a momentous experiment—to permit the Federal Reserve system to focus exclusively on the rate of increase in the money supply, permitting interest rates to move where they would.

The period 1973–1980 was marked not only by indecisive measures to control unit cost inflation but also by a series of efforts to design a national energy policy. The story (well traced out in a Brookings Institution study, *Energy Policy in Perspective*, edited by Craufurd Goodwin) is extremely complex in all its detail. At its core, it can be summarized as follows:

— The Nixon, Ford, and Carter administrations all understood that the U.S. commanded the energy resources to render it essentially independent of oil imports; and they all appreciated that this would have powerful positive effects in both relieving the U.S. balance of payments of a heavy burden and easing, to a degree, the strategic problem posed by the dependence of the advanced industrial world on the continuity of supplies from a volatile and vulnerable Middle East.

— They all understood that a deregulation of oil and natural gas prices was a necessary condition for achieving that objective via its effects in both stimulating energy production and inducing energy conservation.

— However, none of the three presidents ever put the case for these objectives and price policies strongly, steadily, and effectively. Each administration experienced severe internecine struggles on this issue as well as passionate opposition in Congress from representatives of net energy-consuming states and districts.

— Historians can, and no doubt will, argue whether the

American political process as a whole was capable of a better performance; but the upshot was deregulation of the oil price in 1981 and the 1978 legislation on natural gas, of majestic irrational complexity, which promises a still incomplete deregulation by 1985.

— Governmental action to generate a synthetic fuels industry, based on coal and shale, was frustrated during the Ford administration by ambivalence within the administration and opposition in the Congress. It moved forward in the wake of the second oil price jump during the Carter administration, to be radically curtailed in the first two years of the Reagan administration.

— Governmental action to develop a much expanded U.S. coal export capability was weak or nonexistent. Coal production, utilization, and exports increased modestly.

— Nuclear power experienced multiple vicissitudes and moved toward virtual stagnation with seventy-eight plants licensed for commercial operation, as of October 1982; sixty-four construction permits granted; three permits pending; and no reactor units announced since 1978.

— Governmental energy research and development funds were, on the whole, generously supplied, although cut back in the Reagan administration. Their long-run efficacy is still to be assessed.

— None of the three administrations appears to have understood the potentially powerful positive effects on investment and employment, notably in the East and industrial Middle West, of the steady pursuit of a policy of rendering the United States essentially independent of energy imports.

So much for policy. The virtual stagnation of the world economy over the period 1979–1982, combined with the cumulative effects of the relative rise in energy prices on energy conservation, strengthened in the United States by 1975 legislation mandating more fuel-efficient automobiles, yielded a sag in international oil prices. U.S. energy consumption, which had increased at an annual average rate of 4.2 percent in the 1960s, expanded at 0.6 percent in the 1970s and was virtually constant for 1976–1981. U.S. crude and oil imports in 1982 were about 5 million barrels per day, as opposed to more than 8 in 1979. But something like half of this remarkable change was probably due to the deceleration in growth rather than to conservation.

By early 1983, the energy problem, which had enjoyed high priority in the wake of the two oil price jumps of the 1970s, had given way to a concern for unemployment and the size of current and prospective federal deficits. Indeed, in the short run, the possible disruptive as well as positive consequences of a sharp OPEC price decrease formed the major energy issue on the agenda, a matter discussed in chapter 6.

Another strand running through the traumatic 1970s was a gathering awareness that something would have to be done about two aspects of federal policy: the rate of increase in transfer payments for social purposes and the rising pressure on the private sector from the weight of administration of environmental, health, and safety programs. The problems were, of course, quite different.

With respect to transfer payments, as noted earlier, it was clear that the rates of increase of the 1960s and early 1970s could not persist indefinitely. They were absorbing progressively higher proportions of GNP and, at some stage, would have to decelerate. The slowdown in the average rate of real growth after 1973 exacerbated the problem. The U.S. real growth rate between 1961 and 1973 was 4.2 percent; between 1974 and 1982, it was 2.1 percent. The problem was complicated by other factors, for example, the disproportionate increase in medical costs and the surges in outlays for unemployment insurance and other social outlays during the sharp recessions of the latter period. Although not financed from general revenues, the indexing of social security payments and the deceleration of contributions to the social security pool in a period of higher average unemployment (along with the nation's demographic prospects) increased anxiety in both political parties about the long-run viability of the social welfare structure as a whole.

The sharp decline in national security outlays as a proportion of GNP (from 8.9 percent in 1967 to 4.6 percent in 1977) eased this array of problems to a degree (see chart 4). Nevertheless, measures to restrain the rise in transfer payments were undertaken. For example, federal grants to the states, which had risen from 1.3 percent of GNP in 1960 to 3.6 percent in 1975, stabilized at that level. But, after the Soviet invasion of

Afghanistan in 1979, Carter was backed by a consensus that the U.S. defense budget should be increased in real terms, at a fixed rate (5 percent) higher than the expected real rate of increase of GNP. That decision was bound to alter the setting in which allocations to social programs were made, the degree of tension depending on the real rate of growth of the economy.

As for the burdens of excessive centralized administration, the problem was inherent in the drafting of legislation and the setting of operational standards for compliance, especially in the case of environmental and safety and health legislation. The acts of Congress generally defined large, sweeping goals. Administering officials had to try to achieve them in complex, specific circumstances. Rigid loyalty to the language of the legislation could yield costly and burdensome results. The need for weighing costs against benefits came to be recognized in the Ford and Carter administrations, and some measures to strike a more rational balance were undertaken. The task was not easy; and, as the vicissitudes of EPA in 1983 demonstrated, corrective measures could generate results at least as unsatisfactory as the problems they sought to remedy.

A useful critique of U.S. economic policy in the period 1973–1980 must be based on policy concepts different from those actually applied. Those concepts are set out in chapter 5. For the moment, it is sufficient to note the following:

— After, say, mid 1973 the Nixon administration was so bedeviled by the acceleration of the Watergate crisis—by the distraction of the president and the progressive erosion of his authority—that no serious new initiatives could be formulated and implemented.

— The Ford administration, coming to responsibility in the midst of the recession induced by the first oil price explosion, rode out that recession into the recovery of 1976; but it also took no new firm action with respect to the economy in general and to energy in particular.

— The Carter administration's first two years presented an opportunity for a coherent fresh start—in particular, the presentation of the National Energy Plan in April 1977, when the new president's prestige and popular support were at a maximum. Inner conflicts and perceived political conflicts beyond the executive branch produced a plan that was weak, compromised, and in no way matched the rhetoric of "a moral equivalent to war." And this was quickly recognized by Congress and the public. Similarly, incomes policy and other domestic economic initiatives represented inner compromises that failed to yield results that matched the palpable gravity of the problems faced by the country, notably in the wake of the second oil price jump of 1979–1980.

Looked at closely, thought and policy in all three administrations contined to be dominated by those who felt that rapid growth could be reconciled with control over inflation through the manipulation of aggregate demand via fiscal and monetary policy. At its moment of crisis in 1979, the Carter administration backed a particularly rigid version of monetary policy.

The existence of structural problems—for example, energy, excessive rates of increase in transfer payments, excessive federal administrative burdens, inadequate incentives for investment—was recognized, and some actions were initiated. But such initiatives either did not match the scale of the problems to which they were addressed or were overwhelmed by the failure to get at the roots of the problem of stagflation.

Taken as a whole, the period between the presidential elections of 1972 and 1980 was one in which the nation and the world economy confronted a series of difficult, unanticipated problems for which it failed to find coherent, effective responses either in concept or in policy.

3. The Theory of the Counter-Revolution and Its Fatal Flaw

A landslide in a presidential election usually occurs because different forces converge. In the case of the election of November 1980 there was, notably, a convergence of concern about domestic economic disarray and anxiety about the nation's position on the world scene, triggered by the Iranian hostage crisis and the Soviet invasion of Afghanistan, against a background of growing awareness of the relative Soviet arms buildup, which had proceeded during the 1970s as U.S. military expenditures, in real terms, declined.

The American electorate was ready to back a lucid, unambiguous program that promised to come vigorously to grips with underlying problems widely perceived to have spiraled out of control during the period 1973–1980. Mr. Reagan offered such a program.

The Reagan administration began as the most doctrinaire national administration of this century, with the possible exception of Mr. Hoover's. I do not regard the designation "doctrinaire" as inherently pejorative. We all are filled with doctrines, many unexamined. Doctrinaires simply know what they believe and act vigorously to try to bring their doctrines to life.

Mr. Reagan's household contained four kinds of doctrinaires: (1) the supply-siders who wanted to unleash private investment through tax cuts (which would increase the supply of savings and expand private consumption), against a background of reduced regulatory burdens; (2) the budget cutters who wanted to reduce federal outlays for civil purposes, notably social transfer payments, and progressively balance the federal budget on the basis of the expansion of real output and the

increased federal revenues supply-side economics would provide; (3) the monetarists who wanted to squeeze inflation progressively out of the economy by reducing the rate of increase
of the money supply and holding that course until expectations
changed and average money wage increases fell to the level of
the average rate of increase in productivity; and (4) the strategic
planners who wanted to increase sharply the military budget
and create a U.S.-U.S.S.R. balance that might induce Moscow
to accept an evenhanded mutual reduction in arms.

The three economic doctrines were underpinned by a long-
frustrated passion. Since the days of the New Deal a significant
margin of Republican leaders had argued that successive administrations, not excepting moderate Republican administrations, had permitted progressive encroachments on the private
sector which threatened to throttle its vitality. They maintained a strong faith in the virtues of competitive capitalism
and sought to reverse what they perceived to be a half-century's
corrosive trend. Their faith in private enterprise extended to
energy policy, to assistance to developing nations, and to other
fields. As they moved into responsibility, they felt authentically
that their long-delayed chance had come; and they intended to
make the most of it. Part of the support for the supply-siders' tax
cut arose, in fact, from this counter-revolutionary spirit rather
than from a firm belief in supply-side economics. Some held
that a sharp reduction in the federal tax base would force Congress, vulnerable to special interest groups, to cut domestic
spending for social programs. Mr Reagan himself argued that
the way to reduce the profligacy of adolescents was to reduce
their allowances.

These three economic doctrines were clearly enunciated
during Reagan's campaign; and they were subjected to both
critical analysis and skepticism, including George Bush's durable phrase "voodoo economics." But the nation, after a period
of being tossed about by forces it did not control, was disposed
to give someone a chance who seemed to know what he wished
to do. As president, Mr. Reagan remained loyal to his doctrines
for the better part of two years. They were presented with ad-
mirable clarity in the *Economic Report of the President to the
Congress, February 1982*, with its usual statement by the president and elaborate exposition by the Council of Economic Ad-

visers. That document is likely to stand as the authoritative statement of Reaganomics, coming, as it did, before events and pressures in 1982 forced a change of course.

So-called supply-side economics was based on a proposition which, at its extreme, was incontestable—namely, that the progressive transfer of GNP to the public sector via taxes would, at some point, cause a fall in public revenues, as productive activities in the private sector (and the tax revenues they generated) were attenuated. The supply-siders argued that the United States had already passed the point where this corrosive process had taken over. Therefore, a reduction in tax rates would so stimulate the private sector as to yield an increase, rather than a decrease, in public revenues. They often cited Kennedy's policy of 1961–1963, forgetting, however, that Kennedy insisted on a link of wage to productivity increases before proposing a large tax cut. In its pure form the doctrine also asserted that an across-the-board percentage tax cut, evidently favoring those with higher incomes, would increase the supply of savings (and, thus, investment) because, at the margin, the proportion of income saved was higher than the average saved from total income. None of this was judged to be very convincing by experts; it was characterized by Senator Howard Baker as a "riverboat gamble." For example, the proportion of GNP (and taxes) flowing to government was higher in Switzerland and Germany, where private sectors flourished, than in the United States. For example, an increase in private investment depended, above all, on the expected level of real interest rates and output and on the plowback of profits. But the idea of a tax cut commended itself to some, up to a point, without its dubious supply-side refinements. Although the economy was expanding in the first half of 1981, unemployment was still high and capacity utilization low. Moreover, it could be argued that the 1981 tax cut merely compensated for increased social security taxes and the effects of inflation in pushing taxpayers into brackets with higher tax rates.

But the critical assumption made by Reagan—and the fatal flaw in his strategy—was that monetary restraint and a reduction in the rate of inflation were compatible with a simultaneous expansion of the economy induced by tax reduction, diminished administrative burdens on the private sector, and other actions taken by an administration clearly in strong support of the private sector. Without an environment of business expansion, there was a predictable and widely predicted danger that the believed positive effects of the tax cut on investment would not occur, federal revenues would decline, recession-related disbursements would increase, and a disturbing expansion of the federal deficit would take place.

The doctrine of monetary gradualism depended strongly for its validity on a quite particular proposition—that is, that a setting had to be created in which it was a "rational expectation" for business and labor leaders that the money supply would be controlled in terms of stern, inflation-reducing principles translated into an announced rate of increase in the money supply. Under such expectations, business would cease to mark up prices in anticipation of future inflation and labor would accept progressively more modest money wage increases, again on the basis of expected lower future inflation rates. Thus, with price and wage increases rapidly decelerating, the fixed and known rate of increase in the money supply could accommodate the business expansion that the tax cut would induce.

The doctrine of monetary gradualism had no serious basis in theory, history, or recent experience. Recent experience was of particular importance, because business and labor leaders were bound to be strongly influenced by their memories in judging the doctrine and the likely outcome of the policy based on it. When the Reagan administration and the Federal Reserve applied the monetary brakes in July 1981, they initiated the fourth effort in eleven years to use monetary restraint to tame inflation. These experiences were fresh in the minds of those who were being asked to change their expectations: Nixon's (1969–1970), Ford's (1974–1975), and Carter's (1979–1980). All had yielded a surge in interest rates and recession. Business and labor leaders were willing to keep their minds open to the notion that something new was about to happen, but they were mighty skeptical. Few had read the professional literature on "rational expectations," and few would have regarded it as convincing if they did. To the leaders of the private sector of the American economy, the Reagan clampdown was, simply, one in a now familiar sequence of monetarist efforts to master inflation. They had to be shown that it would prove consistent with economic expansion.

As for theory, most monetarists (Milton Friedman excepted) were equally skeptical. The orthodox but candid monetarist Phillip Cagan argued on the basis of a considerable body of empirical research that the core inflation rate could be brought down to zero only by a series of recessions and chronic idle capacity over a period of from a half to almost a full decade. He noted that this required a policy of perseverance and resolve in the face of the political pressures generated by high unemployment that democratic societies had not been able to generate. He was regretfully skeptical of monetarist gradualism but offered no alternative. In effect, Cagan concluded that the only rational expectation was that democratic politicians would be forced by the nature of their profession to reflate the money supply and lower interest rates before major elections.

The redoubtable Frederick Hayek was equally skeptical on the same grounds plus the inherent difficulty in measuring the money supply itself. Hayek advocated, therefore, a Wagnerian solution: a drastic brief depression with unemployment rising to 20 percent, which would end inflation and break the power of the unions once and for all. But even he feared a return of inflation with business revival after his monumental depression.

The flaws in monetary doctrine went deeper, however, than these monetarist observations on how much pain democratic societies could stand and for how long. These flaws all derive from an effort to apply to a complex, interacting economy, in a highly interdependent world, the central monetarist equation, $MV \equiv PQ$. M is the money supply; V is the velocity of its circulation. P is the price level, Q the volume of transactions. PQ is by definition equal to GNP. V cannot be measured directly. It is calculated as a residual by dividing the money stock (M) into GNP (PQ).

The three horizontal lines separating the two sides of the equation indicate that the equation is an identity. This means that, via double-entry bookkeeping, the two sides must always be equal: all the money spent in a given period must equal all the goods and services sold. That is all it tells us.

The equation tells us nothing about causation. It tells us

nothing about the underlying forces determining movements in P and Q. Cost-reducing changes in technology or declines in productivity, the varying fortunes and leverage of OPEC, good and bad harvests have no place in monetary theory. In a magnificent triumph of doctrine over historical experience and common sense, monetary purists argue that such forces affect relative prices but not the price level. Monetary theory is not a theory of growth or a theory of prices or a theory explaining the role of the financial-monetary mechanism in the total workings of the economy. And it applies to a closed economic system, with no role for the interactions of a national economy with the world economic system. All it asserts is that a change in prices or physical output (P or Q) is bound to affect MV; and a change in MV is bound to affect P or Q in some proportion. What the monetary gradualists argued is that, via rational expectations, they could decelerate the money supply in a way that yielded a decline in P while Q expanded.

The three specific flaws flowing from the use of this primitive tool—which remains primitive despite all its apparent refinements—are these.

— First, quite aside from the difficulty in finding an appropriate operational definition for money and accounting for changes in V, it has been historically, and remains down to the present, extremely difficult to fine-tune the money supply. When business confidence exists, there are a variety of ways to expand the money supply even if the monetary authorities seek to temper its expansion, for example, interfirm book credits. When business confidence breaks, marginal changes in the money supply are unlikely to stem the rush for liquidity and the recessionary tide. Action by the monetary authorities has to be sufficiently gross to alter sharply expectations of future business profitability.

— Second, changes in interest rates remain, in fact, the principal means by which monetary policy is implemented. This was recognized in the classic monetary literature (for example, the works of Irving Fisher); but, in their passionate advocacy of control over the money stock (as opposed to interest rate manipulation), modern monetarists have virtually banned from their work reference to interest rates. A sharp rise in interest rates, however, has its initial impact promptly and sharply on certain rather narrow sectors of the economy—at the present time, for example, on housing construction, installment purchases of automobiles, and durable consumer goods. These are, however, closely linked to the basic capital goods industries; and their decline, in turn, suffuses the regions in which they are concentrated and, in a more dilute way, the economy as a whole.

— Third, because it is so oversimplified and unrelated to the economy as a whole, the quantity equation, when used as a guide for policy, fails to capture the side effects of a policy of sustained monetary restraint. Here are some of them. A monetary-induced recession causes a fall in productivity which raises the core rate of inflation (money wage increase minus productivity increase). Thus, in 1969–1970, 1974–1975, 1979–1980, and 1981–1982 unit labor costs (and, therefore, the core inflation rate) were lifted by the monetary-imposed recessions designed to reduce inflation (see chart 3C). Similarly, a rise in interest rates increases housing costs which enter into the cost-of-living index, raising the inflation rate directly, and through cost-of-living adjustments (COLA's) built into contracts and laws affecting the private and public sectors set in motion a further rise in money wages, perpetuating the inflationary thrust. In addition, the succession of recessions cut back the level of investment and contributed to the marked downward trend in productivity, yielding a longer-term inflationary bias in the economy (see chart 3B). Another example: the high interest rates induced by monetary restraint produced an abnormal rise in the dollar on international exchanges as short-term capital flowed to the United States to exploit those higher rates. The strengthened dollar was not justified by relative U.S. costs and prices. Thus, while imports were cheapened by an artificially strong dollar, aiding the fight against inflation, U.S. exports were harder to sell. About one-third of the unemployment and idle capacity of 1981–1982 was caused by the subsidy to imports and the artificial, self-imposed tariff on U.S. exports brought about by the high interest rates induced by monetary policy and the artificial strength they imparted to the dollar via short-term capital flows. In addition, high U.S. interest rates imposed recession on the rest of the world, including financial crisis on many developing countries, further reducing U.S. exports. Above all, monetarists, fastened on the identity which rigidly frames their thought, did not take into account the economic, social, and political costs of the policy they advocated. It may well be that Lindley H. Clark, Jr., the strong, sophisticated, and consistent advocate of monetarism, will prove to be historically correct when he began a piece in the *Wall Street Journal* of January 10, 1983, with the words: "Monetarism may be dead." If so, its death came with the change of Federal Reserve policy in August 1982 which yielded a decline in the discount rate from 16.5 percent to 11.5 percent by November. The causes of the change were the three fundamental flaws cited above, which produced a situation an administration facing a congressional election could not accept and the Federal Reserve Board could no longer defend.

Technically, the experiment with an excessive reliance on a declining rate of increase in the money supply from October 1979 to August 1982 produced one of the most extraordinary anomalies in American economic history: a radical increase in the real rate of interest (see chart 5). The real rate of interest is calculated as the money rate of interest minus the rate of inflation. Subtracting the inflation rate (GNP deflator) from the prime interest rate for the period 1953–1982 yields, down to 1978, a maximum figure of 3.6 percent (1961) and a minimum figure of −1.4 percent (1975). The averages for key periods are as follows:

1953–1960	1.8 percent
1961–1968	2.8 percent
1969–1978	1.5 percent
1979–1982	7.1 percent

The annual figures for the real interest rate since 1979 are also instructive, exhibiting as they do the progressive character of the process:

1979	4.1 percent
1980	6.0 percent
1981	9.5 percent
1982	8.9 percent

That brutal and unprecedented increase in the real rate of interest was the principal instrument for bringing about the acute recession of the period. Some subsidence of real interest rates began in the third quarter of 1982, but as of early 1983

CHART 5. Real Rate of Interest, 1950–1982

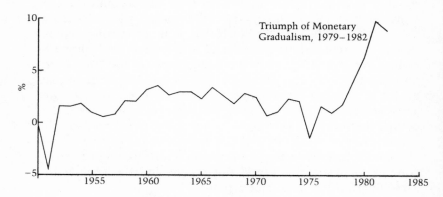

NOTE: The real rate of interest is here taken to be the prime rate minus the rate of change in the GNP deflator.

SOURCE: *Economic Report of the President to the Congress, February 1983,* pp. 166, 240.

they were still about twice as high as in the highest year between 1953 and 1978. A strong, sustained business recovery is difficult to envisage with real interest rates in this high range.

There is a sense in which the intense debate on taxes and expenditures in the Congress in early 1983 concerns alternative theories about how to get the real interest rate down to its normal range, for the conventional view is that it is now kept high because of present and foreseeable federal deficits. In my view, even more is involved—namely, an environment in which it is generally believed that inflation has been brought under control for the long pull, a theme elaborated in chapter 6.

Before moving on, it is worth commenting briefly on the historical studies of the role of money in the economy conducted by monetarists. These studies are relevant to the contemporary debate because many believe they constitute the scientific basis for monetarist policy recommendations. They do not.

For example, Phillip Cagan, after an exhaustive study, concluded that short-run variations in the money stock were caused by cyclical fluctuations in economic activity, including the price changes they induced. The independent dynamic variable was PQ, not M; that is, the money supply, in general, responded passively to the needs of an economy whose dynamics lay outside the terrain monetary theory could illuminate. Moreover, V proved a more volatile variable than monetarists assumed in their concentration on M. And this is the central conclusion of more eclectic analysts of the problem.

It is not widely understood that the leading modern monetarist historians—Friedman, Anna Jacobson Schwartz, and Cagan—did not even attempt to prove that the money supply dominated the course of prices and output. In their scientific work they pause often to assert that the inevitable association of MV and PQ implies nothing about the direction of causation. What they did try to prove is that, historically, money was "important." Specifically, they argued that money was important as an independent variable in only three major respects in the pre-1914 world:

— Wartime inflation.
— The effect of expanded gold production on prices.
— The role of monetary factors in three deep depressions (1875–1878, 1892–1894, 1907–1908).

With respect to wartime inflation, I assume no historian or economist would quarrel with the assertion that prices can be raised by one form or another of money creation in substantial excess of tax collections, notably at a time when manpower and capital are being substantially diverted from productive activities or physically destroyed.

With respect to enlarged gold production, I, at least, would not disagree that it played a role in the price increases of the mid nineteenth century and pre-1914 periods, although I would assign a much less exclusive role to gold than do Friedman and Schwartz, trace out a quite different route of impact, and identify the other, more important nonmonetary forces which imparted an inflationary bias to these periods.

With respect to the three deep depressions cited, I have no doubt that the financial crises which litter the history of the past two centuries played a significant role in the cyclical process. They normally took place after loss of confidence in the profitability of the leading sectors which had carried forward the expansion, that is, after the upper turning point. But the crises and bank failures that then occurred yielded a rush to liquidity reflected in declines in the money supply and high interest rates; and these movements, once under way, reacted back on the level of consumption and investment outlays, output, employment, and prices. But to understand this complex process we must examine the whole interacting economic system, not the monetary supply as a unique initiating force. The upper turning point of business cycles was not, simply, a monetary phenomenon.

As for the depression of the 1930s, monetarists argue that an unwise Federal Reserve policy accounts for the depth and length of the 1929–1933 depression. Broader-based analyses demonstrate that the process was much more complex, involving, among a good many other factors, the pre-1929 decline in housing construction, a prompt collapse in 1930 of automobile sales, a collapse of agricultural prices against a background of excess stocks built up in the 1920s, the Smoot-Hawley tariff, and a failure of the United States to assume a role of leadership in international trade and financial policy.

There is no doubt, either in theory or in experience, that a sharply restrictive monetary policy, acting via increased interest rates and expectations, can induce a recession and that recessions tend quickly to bring down such competitive prices as those of raw materials and gradually reduce money wage rates. One rather striking way to put it (which I owe to Elizabeth Bossong) is that the Reagan administration, despite its formal commitment against administered price control, has, in fact, conducted such control through high real interest rates administered by the Federal Reserve—a policy which comes to bear with peculiar weight on the highly vulnerable capital goods and durable consumer goods industries. The mechanism for price control has been idle industrial capacity and high unemployment.

But there is no reason to believe that monetary policy can be applied in ways which yield a gradual subsidence of prices and wages, as the economy expands; and, most important of all, there is no reason to believe that monetary policy is an instrument capable by itself of providing a long-run framework within which growth can occur in an environment of constant prices. And it is essentially because the Reagan administration came to share that judgment, after painful experience, that it accepted the prospect of a low growth rate and something like a 9–10 percent unemployment level for 1983.

Writing in a Thatcherite rather than a Reaganite context, Sir Ian Gilmour, a former member of the Conservative government, has put the matter very well:

> Had monetarism been a drug, the Committee on the Safety of Medicines would not have allowed anybody to take it, since the claims of its makers had not been proved. Many more tests could have been ordered before it would have been adjudged safe for the market. Until such tests had been concluded, its damaging side-effects would have been considered too certain and its alleged benefits too questionable for it to have gained a certificate of safety. (*Economist*, March 26, 1983, p. 84, review of Ian Gilmour, *Britain Can Work* [Oxford: Martin Robertson])

A colleague once asked why monetarism is so popular when it is patently so deeply flawed. My reply was, simply, that it would be extremely attractive if it worked. Here is a method which claims to reconcile high growth with control over inflation by the action of distant technocrats in a quasiindependent institution, the Federal Reserve. It does not interfere directly with existing institutions for setting prices and wages, and it takes responsibility and authority off the shoulders of politicians. But neither recent experience, theory, nor history justified President Reagan's hope for monetarist gradualism which he expressed with such clarity in his February 1982 *Economic Report*:

> I have made clear my support for a policy of gradual and less volatile reduction in the growth of the money supply. Such a policy will ensure that inflationary pressures will continue to decline without impairing the operation of our financial markets as they mobilize savings and direct them to their most productive uses. It will also ensure that high interest rates, with their large inflation premiums, will no longer pose a threat to the well-being of our housing and motor vehicle industries, to small business and farmers, and to all who rely upon

the use of credit in their daily activities. In addition, reduced monetary volatility will strengthen confidence in
monetary policy and help lower interest rates.

As chapter 4 details, the failure of this doctrine in 1981–
1982 destroyed the hopes of the supply-siders and the budget
balancers and created domestic political pressures on the military budget which endangered the hopes of those who aimed
to negotiate an evenhanded radical reduction in U.S.-Soviet
strategic arms.

4. The Counter-Revolutionaries at Work: 1981–1983

History does not unfold with the clarity of abstract concepts or even as a simple clash of concepts. New policies, if they are to be designed and implemented, must start from a base in 1983. Table 2 sets out annual figures for 1979–1982 and quarterly figures from the third quarter of 1980, covering some of the key economic variables of this period.

The business-cycle pattern is clear enough: from a peak plateau in the first half of 1979 the economy moved into a recession which bottomed out in mid 1980. A slow and incomplete recovery of about a year followed which ended with the clamping on of the money supply brakes in the summer of 1981. A deeper recession then occurred which continued to December 1982. A process of expansion was under way early in 1983.

Against this background, the following specific features of table 2 should be noted.

1. The recovery of 1979–1980, aborted in mid 1981 by monetary policy, failed to yield a substantial increase in employment and only a modest increase in capacity utilization, after which both plunged to record postwar levels.

2. The limited but real subsidence of inflation and interest rates in the course of 1982 failed to yield a fall in the real interest rate until the last two quarters of 1982, but it was still (8.3 percent) more than twice its maximum normal level as 1983 began.

3. As after the first oil price jump of 1973–1974, money wage increases subsided under the impact of both decelerating inflation (in part caused by a fall in real oil prices) and high unemployment. The low point for money wage increases in the

TABLE 2. The Course of the U.S. Economy, 1979–1983

Year		Prime Rate	Rate of Change of Price Level (GNP Deflator)	Real Interest Rate[a]	Real GNP Growth Rate	Un- employ- ment Rate	Capacity Utili- zation	Comper sation p Hour[b]
1979		12.7%	8.6%	4.1%	2.8%	5.8%	85.7%	9.3%
1980		15.3	9.3	6.0	−0.4	7.0	79.1	10.2
1981		18.9	9.4	9.5	1.9	7.5	78.5	9.7
1982		14.9	6.0	8.9	−1.8	9.5	69.8	7.3
1980	III	11.7	9.6	2.1	1.6	7.7	75.9	10.4
	IV	16.6	10.5	6.1	4.3	7.4	79.1	9.8
1981	I	19.5	10.9	8.6	7.9	7.4	79.9	11.9
	II	19.0	6.8	12.2	−1.5	7.4	79.8	7.2
	III	20.2	9.0	11.2	2.2	7.4	79.3	9.0
	IV	17.2	8.8	8.4	−5.3	8.4	74.8	7.4
1982	I	16.2	4.3	11.9	−5.1	8.8	71.6	7.9
	II	16.5	4.6	11.9	2.1	9.3	70.3	6.0
	III	14.7	5.0	9.7	0.7	9.8	64.7	6.6
	IV	12.0	3.7	8.3	−2.5	10.5	67.6	5.5
1983	I	11.0	5.8	5.2	3.1	10.2		6.1

Output per Hour[b]	Unit Labor Cost[b]	Real Compensation per Hour[b]	Energy Prices[c]	Food, etc., Prices[c]	Federal Deficit Calendar Years National Income and Product Accounts ($ Billions)	International Balance on Current Accounts ($ Billions) Trade Balance	International Balance on Current Accounts ($ Billions) Overall Balance	Dollar Exchange Rate (March 1973 = 100)
−1.3%	10.7%	−1.7%	37.4%	10.0 %	−16.1	−27.3	−0.5	88.1
−0.9	11.2	−2.9	18.1	10.1	−61.4	−25.3	1.5	87.4
1.4	8.1	−0.7	11.9	4.3	−60.0	−27.9	4.5	102.9
0.2	7.1	1.1	1.3	3.2	−149.5	−36.3	—	116.6
3.4	6.8	2.5	2.4	18.4	−73.1	−3.9	3.4	85.4
3.1	6.5	−2.8	−0.4	12.4	−65.2	−5.2	0.9	89.0
4.9	6.6	1.2	40.8	2.4	−39.7	−4.3	3.2	94.5
−1.2	8.4	−1.2	14.4	—	−40.5	−6.5	1.4	103.1
−0.3	9.4	−2.7	2.8	10.4	−58.0	−7.8	0.7	110.1
−3.4	11.2	−0.2	−2.4	3.6	−101.7	−9.2	−0.9	105.4
0.7	7.2	4.8	−8.4	4.0	−118.4	−5.9	1.0	109.9
0.9	5.1	0.7	12.4	6.8	−119.6	−5.8	2.2	114.0
0.4	3.1	−1.1	5.2	0.8	−156.0	−12.5	−5.2	119.8
2.7	5.1	3.5	−4.0	0.8	−204.2	−12.1	−6.1	122.2
4.8	1.3	6.5	−2.4	0.2	—	—	—	—

[a] The real interest rate is calculated by subtracting the rate of inflation (in this case, the GNP deflator) from the interest rate (in this case, the prime rate charged by banks). The quarterly GNP deflator percentages are quarter-to-quarter changes and, therefore, do not average to the figure for the annual rate of change.

[b] Nonfarm business sector.

[c] Changes in consumer prices, at annual rates.

SOURCE: *Economic Report of the President to the Congress, February 1983; Economic Indicators*, December 1982 and April 1983, prepared for the Joint Economic Committee by the Council of Economic Advisers.

first case was 6.6 percent in the fourth quarter of 1975. The low point thus far, after the second oil price jump, was 6 percent in the fourth quarter of 1982. Output per hour turned negative in all three recessions (1974–1975, 1979–1980, 1981–1982), but it revived as the recession bottomed out and recovery began. The low point for unit labor costs—the core inflation rate— came, in the first case, in the second and third quarters of 1975 (when it was briefly negative); it was down to 3.1 percent in the third quarter of 1982. Although this book would regard the course taken by the Reagan administration as unwise, the strongest case for the imposition of a monetary-induced recession in mid 1981 was that the rate of increase of unit labor costs rose from its December 1980 low to 9.3 percent in the third quarter of 1981. This was mainly due, however, not to a rise in money wage increases, which were subsiding, but to a 6.2 percent negative shift in the impact of productivity on unit labor costs between the first and second quarters of 1981 (from 4.9 percent to −1.3 percent). Thus, unlike its three predecessors since 1969, Reagan's monetary-induced recession of 1981–1982 was initiated in an environment of decelerating rather than accelerating inflation.

4. The erratic downward course of food and energy prices from 1979 to 1982 played a significant role in damping the overall inflation rate. The recessions of that period played a minor role in the behavior of food prices, a more substantial (perhaps 50 percent) role in cutting the demand for energy. The decline in other industrial raw material prices was almost wholly a result of the recession.

5. The federal deficit increased in the usual way as tax receipts fell and social outlays rose in the recession of 1979–1980; narrowed with the recovery of 1980–1981; and then moved to unprecedented levels with the convergence of the tax cuts of 1981, increased military and interest outlays, and the acute recession of 1981–1982.

6. The merchandise trade balance remained strongly negative, despite recession. Imports were damped by recession, weakened oil prices, and the rising value of the dollar; but exports were also damped by the strong dollar and the global character of the recession, notably in 1981–1982. From the

third quarter of 1982 the overall balance, cushioned hitherto by services (including net capital flows), turned negative.

7. Real wages in the nonfarm business sector declined between 1979 and 1982; farm income declined in real terms from $14.9 billion (1967 dollars) in 1979 to $5.9 billion in the third quarter of 1982; total real per capita consumption expenditures were lower in the third quarter of 1982 than in 1979, as was the level of gross investment, measured in real terms.

This brisk portrait of an economic system in extreme disarray is, as is conventional, set out in aggregate terms embracing the American economy as a whole. It is incomplete in three major respects.

First, the impact of the briefly interrupted recessions of 1979–1982 struck the regions of the country unequally. The range of unemployment rates in the ten most populous states in November 1982 was, for example, between 17.2 percent for Michigan and 7.2 percent for Massachusetts.

Second, this spectrum related directly to the linkage of the regions to dynamic sectors of the economy or to weak or degenerating sectors. Regions caught up in expanding sectors, incorporating new, rapidly diffusing technologies (for example, Massachusetts), did relatively well, as did regions which were net energy exporters (for example, Texas and the Mountain states). The latter, however, were promptly affected by the subsidence of energy prices in 1981–1982. On the other hand, the industrial Middle West was extremely hard hit because of its deeply rooted linkage to motor vehicles, steel, machine tools, rubber, and so on, and a number of the inner cities within the region experienced accelerated decay.

Third, the recession cut state and local revenues and, therefore, expenditures. Corrected for inflation, they were running at a lower rate in the fourth quarter of 1982 than in 1979. This constraint, at a time of continued increase in population, came against a background of prior deceleration. Between 1961 and 1973, state and local expenditures had averaged a 4.2 percent annual increase in real terms. Between 1973 and 1979, the figure was 2.9 percent. This deceleration and decline were the basis for the buildup of the large physical infrastructure deficit of which Americans became conscious in 1982. Hard-pressed state and local governments balanced their books, as the law requires, by living off capital—that is, postponing investments to maintain and to expand, in response to population growth, basic infrastructure and essential services (see chart 10). In this respect also, the United States was a poorer country early in 1983 than it was in 1979.

In one area the counter-revolution achieved a portion of its objectives—that is, an increase in national defense expenditures as a proportion of GNP—but the expansion was seriously threatened by the Reagan administration's economic policy, which created a corrosive political conflict between the common defense and the general welfare. Another objective was only partially achieved—that is, a reduction in civil expenditures by the federal government. There were reductions, notably in energy, natural resources and the environment, housing credits, transportation, and community and regional development. Outlays for foreign aid shared in that decline. But high interest rates and the recession itself forced an unwelcome increase in interest payments on the federal debt as well as for unemployment benefits and certain other income security outlays. The rather odd result, for an administration dedicated to the proposition that the role of the federal government in the economy should be reduced, was a rise of over 1 percent of GNP devoted to transfer payments (excepting interest), of about 3 percent for federal spending as a whole.

This account of what transpired in recent years is incomplete in another respect—that is, the vicious circle in which the world economy is caught up. As the largest of the world's economies, the United States is, in part, the cause of the process, imposing recession on others. But most other governments have also been trying to deal with the problems they confront with inadequate macroeconomic tools, and this has contributed to a situation bluntly described in the November–December 1982 issue of the German economic journal *Inter Economics*:

> . . . the weakness of growth accompanied by international payments crises is causing a world-wide increase in unemployment. An attempt is being made to combat the crisis with domestic instruments and a more or less well

disguised beggar-thy-neighbour policy, including protectionist practices. Followed on a world-wide scale, this
policy is doomed to failure. It leads to a reduction of
world trade and of the international division of labour.
This only weakens the growth of real income even further and the vicious circle is complete.

The process has two interacting dimensions: economic relations among the advanced industrial countries of the OECD
and the interaction of the OECD countries and the developing
world of Latin America, Asia, and Africa.

As of the third or fourth quarter of 1982, unemployment
was 12.7 percent in Canada, 8.7 percent in France, 6.2 percent
in West Germany, 4.5 percent in Italy, 13 percent in the United
Kingdom and 10.5 percent in the United States. In Japan, it had
risen only from 2.2 percent in 1981 to 2.4 percent. The growth
rate of the advanced industrial countries, averaging 5.1 percent
in 1960–1973, 2.7 percent in 1974–1979, averaged 0.7 percent in 1980–1982, −0.5 percent for the latter year. With the
growth engine of the 1950s and 1960s turned off (that is, the
rapid rise in consumers' real incomes), the advanced industrial
nations have sought either to expand employment by increased
exports or to prevent further increases in unemployment by
impeding imports. Thus, de facto trade barriers are rising and
ugly diplomatic conflicts are taking place across both the Atlantic and the Pacific as well as between Western Europe and
Japan. Behind those conflicts are deeply rooted domestic political pressures which are, evidently, capable of driving a stagnant
world trading system into self-defeating beggar-thy-neighbor
policies. There is no political leader who does not understand
the strategic as well as economic dangers of this course; but
when U.S. automobile workers demand protection from Japanese imports and Japanese farmers march in protest against increased U.S. agricultural imports, Jefferson's "firebell in the
night" is ringing.

Meanwhile, a second corrosive interaction was under way
in 1980–1982. In the wake of the first oil price jump, the momentum of the more advanced developing countries was fairly
well maintained by greatly enlarged private borrowing and
some increases in foreign aid from the OECD countries. The

real growth rate of the developing countries as a whole was 5.4 percent in 1955–1970, 5.3 percent for 1970–1980. The combination of high interest rates and the sharp OECD recession after 1979 brought a good many of them to acute crisis. The real growth rate for developing countries was down to 2.2 percent in 1981, with a negative figure for Latin America. They simply could not earn enough foreign exchange in a depressed world economy to meet their commitments to repay interest and principal. Several major oil exporters found themselves in a similar position. They borrowed heavily in the 1970s on the assumption that the real oil price would continue to rise, and they were thrown into acute disarray by the combination of the oil price decline and the global recession. The IMF, the central banks, and the major private banks have wisely moved as a kind of consortium to roll over the debts of those countries. The price has been a commitment to conduct more austere economic policies, that is, policies of lower real growth.

Here the process takes another costly turn. By and large, the growth rates of the developing regions have been higher than those of the advanced industrial countries. Therefore, their role in world trade has risen. In 1965, for example, the developing countries absorbed 27 percent of the world's imports; in 1981, they absorbed 31 percent. For the United States the shift is even more striking. In 1973, 29 percent of U.S. exports went to developing countries; in the first three quarters of 1981, 38 percent. Thus, the painfully exacted commitments to slow growth or stagnation in the developing nations have reduced sharply potential U.S. export markets which, under normal circumstances, would rapidly expand.

But even greater dangers are embedded in the present low-level trap into which the developing regions have been driven. The stage at which their demographic and growth dynamics now stand demands high growth rates as a minimum condition for reasonable political and social stability. Prolonged low growth or stagnation is likely to trigger societal crises with significant strategic consequences.

There is little set out thus far in this chapter which was not widely understood by early 1983. And after the congressional elections of November 1982—with the run-up to the presidential election in 1984 clearly in the minds of political leaders—strong pressures to alter the policies of the Reagan administration developed.

The emerging consensus among Republicans had these simple but powerful elements:

— Interest rates had to be brought down; and this demanded not only a more expansionist Federal Reserve policy, which was already under way, but also a reduction in the prospective federal deficit. The latter, it was believed, would not only generate expectations that interest rates and the inflation rate would begin to rise again, but, in fact, the borrowing requirements to cover the prospective federal deficit (estimated as more than 6 percent of GNP for 1983) would crowd out private borrowers and, on a straight supply-demand market basis, drive up interest rates and throttle any recovery that might develop in 1983–1984.

— To narrow the federal deficit, all three of the following forms of action were required: a reduction in the rate of growth of military spending, some further reduction in the civil outlays of government, and an increase of taxes.

Anxieties about the U.S.-Soviet arms balance and the U.S. negotiating position in arms control negotiations set a limit on the reduction in military expenditures. Public opinion was beginning to set a limit on further reductions in social welfare expenditures, notably in an environment of continued high unemployment and widespread human distress. Therefore, if the deficit was to be brought and held under, say, $100 billion, a tax increase was required.

The consensus was by no means universal among Republicans. Those with residual faith in supply-side economics argued that recovery in 1983–1984 would be more rapid than the administration envisaged and that the federal deficit would be less than projected. The administration should, therefore, keep the faith and avoid a tax increase. This was evidently Mr. Reagan's instinct. In straightforward Keynesian terms, no doubt reaching back to his memory of the 1930s, he expressed the view that a period of recession was a bad time to raise taxes; but he came under strong pressure from Republican leaders to pursue a more conventional conservative course and to narrow the budget deficit by all possible means, including a tax increase. His State of the Union message of January 25,

1983, compromised the matter with a cosmetic proposal for a delayed, contingent future tax increase, most unlikely to survive in a Congress jealous of its control over the nation's purse strings, reluctant to commit a future Congress.

Reagan began with a belief that a soft fiscal policy could be combined with a hard monetary policy. The reconciliation did not happen. The hard money policy won. The result was two-fold: an unacceptable rise in the federal deficit, further softening fiscal policy, and an unacceptable rise in unemployment which forced a softening of monetary policy. In combination, the soft fiscal and monetary policies helped set in motion a recovery. The official projection for policy and the economy was a slow expansion that would avoid a reacceleration of interest rates and the inflation rate with, no doubt, the hope that a more robust recovery would be brought about in 1984 as a backdrop for the November election of that year. Given the backlog of repressed demand for housing, automobiles, durable consumer goods, and weakening oil prices, the recovery might be somewhat stronger in the first instance than officially projected. But its foundations were universally judged by reasonably objective observers to be infirm on several grounds: a probable weakening of the dollar, as interest rates fell, would raise import prices; recovery itself would raise raw material prices and, in time, stiffen energy prices; a new program to relieve the distress of farmers by cutting acreage would raise agricultural prices; the large prospective federal deficits would prevent a decline of real interest rates to normal levels and might, indeed, yield before long an inhibiting rise in interest rates before unemployment was greatly reduced and capacity utilization lifted to prosperity levels; and, above all, high levels of unemployment would have to be maintained to prevent a resurgence of wage-push inflation.

Among the Democrats there was no lucid consensus or, even, clear-cut division of opinion on the budget and taxes; and that was a luxury they could afford as an opposition party. Their time of truth would come in 1984 when they sought to take over the White House. For the moment, they appeared content to oppose further cuts in social expenditures, to urge deeper cuts in military expenditures, and to advocate one form or another of public works programs to reduce unemployment—a proposal to which Reagan acceded, to a degree, early in 1983. Some urged that the prospective tax cut, to go into effect on July 1, 1983, be forgone. The Democrats generally joined the Republicans late in 1982 in passing a rise in the tax on gasoline to finance a $33 billion program of road repair against the background of a minimum estimate of $315 billion required for this purpose. And they joined the Republicans in backing the consensus in the bipartisan panel to maintain the viability of the social security system.

I would also note a new strand in the Democratic portion of the economic report of the Joint Economic Committee. The bulk of the argument is couched in conventional macroeconomic terms—that is, fiscal and monetary policy. But there is the suggestion of support for an incomes policy in the vice-chairman's observation (Lee H. Hamilton): "A better way to hold down the wage-price spiral would be to forge a consensus anti-inflation policy based on the cooperation of business, labor, and government." The proposition is again stated in Recommendation No. 17 of the report. It remains to be seen if the Democratic party as a whole will build on this lead.

Influential Democratic economists took various positions, some a good deal like those taken by moderate Republicans, with one exception: they generally refused to regard the prospective 1983 deficit with equivalent alarm; argued for the primacy of recovery; and asserted that only a strong recovery could narrow the federal deficit. Several suggested an incomes policy was necessary—that is, a direct approach to reducing hard-core inflation via the restraint of wages, salaries, and dividends. This, they argued, would permit a faster recovery with less inflation; but, without elaborating how this might be done, they quickly set it aside as politically unthinkable until after the next presidential election.

There is one major exception to this generalization, Felix Rohatyn. As a banker of wide practical knowledge of the state of economic affairs at home and abroad, having led the effort to pull New York City back from bankruptcy and having escaped the deformities of a formal education in mainstream economics, he has advocated systematically in this period a pragmatic series of measures, some of which are similar to those set out in chapter 6.

Three broad observations can be made about the changes in course and the debates of early 1983.

First, the major issues debated within the two major parties, between them, and in the media were almost wholly in terms of the manipulation of macrodemand. With the shift in the Federal Reserve to a policy of expanded money supply and lowered interest rates, in support of recovery, the argument became almost pure Keynesian—that is, an argument about taxes and expenditures. At some risk of oversimplification, it came down to the view that the federal deficit must be narrowed immediately, at the bottom of recession, or recovery could not proceed, versus the view that the deficit could be narrowed only by the process of recovery itself and, that, therefore, the large prospective 1983 deficit should, more or less, be accepted.

Second, neither Republican nor Democratic political leaders offered a policy that could reconcile a return to rapid and sustained growth with inflation under control and low real interest rates guaranteed for the long pull. With monetarist gradualism in general disrepute and with extreme anxiety about both the level of unemployment and the scale of the federal deficit, the debate was about alternative Keynesian paths to recovery. But well-founded anxieties about a future rise in interest rates and revived inflation remained a major bar to a strong, confident recovery.

Third, in both Reagan's assessment of the State of the Union in January 1983 and that of the Democratic party, certain new issues surfaced—for example, the implication of new emerging technologies for research and development outlays, education, and labor retraining. There also seemed to be a growing awareness of the scale of the infrastructure problem facing the United States. Except for a proposed rise in federal outlays in support of science, the treatment was cosmetic in the one case, impressionistic in the other. Nevertheless, this widening of the public agenda was a wholesome development. But serious actions to come to grips with these and other basic economic issues dealt with in chapter 6 clearly awaited the crystallization of a policy which would reconcile rapid growth with reliable long-term control over inflation. Neither the Reagan administration nor the Democrats faced up to that central question.

We turn now, therefore, to remedy for a situation of virtual intellectual and policy bankruptcy in the two major political parties.

5. Concepts for a Civilized Synthesis

The concepts required to illuminate the path to sustained, high, noninflationary growth deal with variables systematically ignored or set aside for ad hoc observations by mainstream macroeconomists: technology and its relation to the structure of the working force; the dynamics of the rise, decline, and rehabilitation of industries; the process of generating adequate supplies of basic commodities, including clean air and water; the provision and maintenance of an adequate physical infrastructure; and the institutional methods by which wages in major industries are set. It is in these domains that both our major unsolved problems and possibilities lie.

This chapter begins with a brief evocation of the probable effects on the economy of a return to a regular high growth rate. It then asks: is, in fact, high regular growth possible in the 1980s and 1990s? If so, what sectors would lead and carry forward the growth process? Finally, we confront the critical question: can a strong recovery be sustained without a revival of inflation?

The Virtues of High Sustained Growth

Now what would a high regular growth rate do for the American economy?

We start with unemployment at 10–11 percent, capacity utilization under 70 percent, and real output at least some $300 billion short of what it would be at 6 percent unemployment and 85 percent capacity utilization. Those are, incidentally, modest targets for "full employment." I believe the U.S. should aim for lower unemployment and higher capacity utilization;

as will emerge, serious investment requirements of the U.S. economy and the world economy as a whole demand such an intense sustained effort.

Given the rate of growth of the working force and the underlying potential rate of productivity increase, a high, sustained rate of growth will be required if unemployment is rapidly to decline. A conventional macroestimate for such an optimistic high-growth scenario is for real GNP growth of about 7 percent for several years, gradually subsiding to 4 percent as relatively full employment and capacity utilization are achieved. The unemployment rate might drop at something like 2 percent each year. That kind of powerful, sustained growth would itself bring the federal deficit down from over 6 percent of GNP for fiscal year 1983 to, say, 1.3 percent. A 1.3 percent deficit at the present time would be a relatively modest $40 billion.

If such a powerful boom were mounted, an increase in federal tax rates might be required as full employment and capacity utilization were approached, both to constrain inflation and to permit a balanced federal budget.

It cannot be too strongly emphasized that only rapid, sustained growth is capable of increasing federal revenues, cutting unemployment benefits and related expenditures, supplying the underpinnings for the maintenance of civilized social services and an adequate national defense.

Rapid, sustained growth would have other significant effects, beyond the reduction of unemployment and the narrowing of the federal deficit. As full capacity utilization was approached, long-term private investment in new plant and equipment would resume, lifting productivity and strengthening the nation's competitive position on the world scene. As unemployment fell, the resistance of labor to the installation of new technologies (for example, robots) would also diminish. As for the nation's obsolescing infrastructure, the resources for their rehabilitation would automatically flow into the treasuries of state and local governments as steady, rapid growth resumed, while rising real incomes would enlarge the pool available for both public and private savings, including the increased cash flows in the private sector available for the plowback of profits into investment.

Internationally, such growth would lift the economies of the advanced industrial world as well as the developing regions, easing the now precarious debt situation of the latter. All this would have positive playback effects on U.S. exports. It would also diminish protectionist pressures in the United States (and elsewhere); and, with a gradual lifting of anxieties in American communities, it would permit the Congress to approach problems of foreign aid and North-South economic relations in terms of enlightened long-run self-interest rather than the short-run constraints imposed by severe recession at home.

Will the New Technologies Cause Chronic High Unemployment?

We come now to closely linked questions: is such a phase of high, sustained growth possible; and would it rapidly bring down the level of unemployment? Macroeconomists do not pose these questions. They assume that a sufficiently high level of private and public expenditure will automatically yield this outcome. They do not concern themselves with how consumers spend their incomes, where investment flows, or whether current technologies will permit the whole working force to be employed. They judge that normal market processes will look after these matters more or less rationally and automatically.

In fact, every business expansion has its own character, marked by certain sectors which exhibit particularly rapid rates of increase. In American history, for example, there have been booms led by the expansion of cotton textiles, cotton or wheat acreage, railroads, steel, and automobiles, among others. As noted earlier, the extraordinary expansion of the advanced industrial world in the 1950s and 1960s was led by the diffusion of the private automobile, durable consumer goods, the migration to suburbia, and disproportionately high rates of increase in outlays on higher education, health, and travel. These, in turn, depended on a phase of relatively declining basic commodity prices and, therefore, rising real incomes, as well as on the existence of a large, hitherto unapplied backlog of technologies for Western Europe and Japan and a range of new technologies available for all.

The initial phase of the business expansion begun in early 1983 is likely to be led by inventory restocking, including outlays for housing, automobiles, and durable consumer goods postponed by the protracted regime of high interest rates in 1979–1982.

But if one thing is certain, it is that a sustained boom of the 1980s and 1990s will have different leading sectors than the boom of the 1950s and 1960s. As I shall argue, the world economy cannot count on another protracted period of relatively falling basic commodity prices; and, in any case, the automobile sectoral complex in the advanced industrial countries was already decelerating rapidly in the late 1960s. As macroeconomics assumes, conventional competitive markets will, up to a point, look after the leading sectors if adequate levels of effective demand are sustained and real interest rates are in a normal range. But the appropriate structure of the boom, as I envisage it, requires widespread awareness of its component elements as well as strands of public policy not required in the great expansion of the 1950s and 1960s.

Clearly, one component in a boom of the 1980s and 1990s will be the diffusion of a range of major new technologies. Here we confront a question which is the subject of a widespread anxiety in all the advanced industrial countries: will the emerging technologies of what I shall call the Fourth Industrial Revolution yield chronic high technological unemployment? I include in the Fourth Industrial Revolution innovations in microelectronics, communications, the offshoots of genetics, the laser, robots, and new synthetic materials.

It may be useful to begin a response to that question by making clear both the oversimplification and the element of reality involved in the notion that inventions and innovations come in groups which justify the designation of a sequence of definable industrial revolutions.

By no means do all innovations come in such grand clusters. To start at the less glamorous end of the spectrum, a great deal of invention and innovation of great importance has gone on since the 1780s which consists of incremental improvements in existing technologies. Some of these incremental improvements find their way into patent records, many do not. The rates of productivity increase we observe in history are significantly determined by this kind of endemic, incremental invention and innovation. The path of this kind of refinement by small steps is subject to diminishing returns, as particular technologies age and potentialities for improvement decline.

Second, innovations of varying significance, creating new industries, large and small, are initiated, in modern times, over a wide front; and they are by no means all related to each other. One authority has identified, for example, seventeen substantial innovations, rooted in technologies and processes known before 1914, which played an important part in the interwar years. They range from aircraft to ball bearings to more efficient office machinery and canning methods. A more recent study lists sixty-two innovations for the period 1920–1970. They range from the zip fastener, the ball-point pen, and cinerama to electronic digital computers, DDT, and synthetic fibers.

But economic historians and some economists have recognized that, in addition, there have been, before our time, three giant innovational clusters: factory-manufactured textiles, Cort's method for making iron from coke, and Watt's steam engine, all of which came on stage in a substantial way in Britain of the 1780s; then the railroads, making considerable commercial headway in the 1830s but generating substantial booms in Britain, the American Northeast, and Germany in the 1840s and leading on to the revolution in steelmaking in the 1870s; finally, electricity, a new batch of chemicals, and the internal-combustion engine. These became significant round about the opening of the twentieth century and, in its various elaborations, carried economic growth forward through the 1960s in the advanced industrial countries. This grouping of innovational giants has still a good deal to commend it, although it is, of course, highly oversimplified.

Since the dating of the initiation of these clusters is arbitrary, one could adjust them to, say, a sixty- or seventy-year periodicity; but there is no rational reason to assume a uniform rhythm for such grand innovational cycles.

The question before us is: what are the employment implications of the batch of technologies I have designated as the Fourth Industrial Revolution? There are four questions to pose and try to answer:

— How big will the new industries become?
— How many will they employ and unemploy?
— What mix of skills will they require?
— And, above all, are other likely or possible demands for labor in the advanced industrial economies capable of keeping the working force, over the whole spectrum of skills, fully employed?

I have recently tried to find in the current literature approximate answers to the first three questions, with rather thin results. Part of the problem is that it is difficult to measure the size and employment characteristics of even an old innovational complex. What we need are data on all the output of goods and services and all the employment generated by a given industrial complex. The American automobile industry is the best-documented case we have. As of 1972, the industry, broadly but still incompletely defined, employed in the United States over 5 million people. Of those, only 16 percent helped manufacture motor vehicles; 2 percent were in petroleum refining, 11 percent in wholesaling, 32 percent in retailing, 8 percent in repair and other services, 27 percent in transportation. These calculations do not include employment in producing steel and other inputs for motor vehicle manufacture. Overall, in 1972 something like 18 percent of GNP was generated by this complex.

It is unlikely that the innovations of the Fourth Industrial Revolution will generate quite so impressive a range and scale, although one set of calculations (table 3) for the United States estimates a 1990 total employment of 2.45 million in the following high-technology sectors: robot production; laser processing; handling of new synthetic materials; genetic engineering; bionic medical electronics; laser, holographic, and optical maintenance. I cite this figure simply to suggest that, since the new technologies are likely to suffuse a wide range of sectors, employment within them could become quite large over the next generation or so, depending on the rate at which the technologies are diffused.

Indeed, on a broader definition of high-technology manufacturing sectors, employment increased at an average annual rate of 1.8 percent from 1965 to 1979, other manufacturing at 0.6 percent, total manufacturing employment at 1.1 percent. In

TABLE 3. Sectors with High Employment Growth Prospects

Occupation	Estimated Employment, 1990
Industrial-robot production	800,000
Geriatric social work	700,000
Energy technicians	650,000
Industrial-laser processing	600,000
Housing rehabilitation	500,000
Handling new synthetic materials	400,000
On-line emergency medical	400,000
Hazardous-waste management	300,000
Genetic engineering	250,000
Bionic medical electronics	200,000
Laser, holographic, and optical-fiber maintenance	200,000

SOURCE: This estimate, from the Labor Department and other sources, was published in *Newsweek*, October 18, 1982, p. 83.

the business expansion of 1975–1979 the relative rates were 4.6 percent, 2.7 percent, and 3.5 percent, respectively. In 1979 40 percent of all manufacturing employment was in the high-technology sectors. Clearly, a structural shift to high-technology manufacturing sectors, however defined, is already under way.

For our purposes, however, I would underline two narrower points. First, as the motor vehicle complex suggests, manufacturing employment is only a modest proportion of the total employment generated by an innovational industry. All manner of workers—not merely Ph.D.'s and engineers—can find employment in innovational complexes when they move from the laboratory into the economy. A recent pamphlet of the U.S. Department of Labor contains an article on employment prospects in the computer industry which captures this point, in a brisk summary in the table of contents, with a vivid, if rather odd, analogy: "Computers—key weapons in the Post-Industrial Revolution—need an army-sized work-force to keep them aimed, loaded, and firing. The duties of these troops are so varied that almost anyone can find a place in their ranks." Moreover, the evidence thus far is that the introduction of computers into business and government offices may well increase the efficiency of a firm's operations as a whole, but it is not likely to reduce the demand for clerical workers. To some degree, a change in skills is required; but this does not appear to have posed formidable problems.

Second, a point memorably made by Adam Smith's homily on pin manufacture and vindicated by more than two centuries of economic history down to a highly efficient electronics plant in the Watts section of Los Angeles: large-scale production permits not only specialization of function but also the productive employment of relatively unskilled labor.

From what we now know, I find it difficult to believe that the computer revolution, in most of its applications, will generate serious problems of chronic technological unemployment. Robots are a different matter, and I suspect they are the component in the Fourth Industrial Revolution that lies at the heart of a great deal of the anxiety about technology and future employment prospects.

Here are instruments which directly replace men and women in manufacturing, a sore-beset component of the advanced industrial economies of the West. At an outer limit, one study suggests that, over twenty years, nonservo-controlled robots could replace up to 1 million workers in the United States while servo-controlled robots could replace up to 3 million out of a total of about 8 million operative workers in manufacturing. The automotive, electrical equipment, machinery, and fabricating metals industries are the likely candidates for this process.

Replacement, of course, does not mean displacement. Robots require not only operators but also workers to manufacture, program, and maintain the equipment. No satisfactory estimates appear to exist on the numerical balance of jobs replaced and created. What seeems to emerge is that retraining is not a difficult process for robot operation; maintenance requires considerably higher skill levels; manufacture and programming require quite advanced engineering and computer virtuosity. On balance, the most likely outcome of the diffusion of the robot is the net displacement of less skilled workers or workers so near to retirement that firms may not be willing to invest in retraining. It will also generate a heightened demand for engineers and computer programmers. Depending on the pace at which robot diffusion proceeds, the scale of the problem posed by the net displacement of less skilled or unretrained workers could be substantial, although, to the extent that it permitted greater competitiveness and higher total output in the industries where robots were installed, that net displacement would be narrowed.

My tentative response to the first three questions I posed is, then:

— The new industries could get to be quite large by historical standards, because the technologies they incorporate are potentially ubiquitous; but the flimsy evidence available does not permit confident prediction about the pace of diffusion and their ultimate scale.

— Therefore, we simply do not know how many members of the working force they will employ and unemploy.

— But the mix of skills required in the innovational complexes as a whole is likely to be wide; and, with large-scale production, the skill requirements in manufacture are likely to diminish.

If these tentative judgments prove true, the expansion of these industries is unlikely to be impeded for long by skilled-labor bottlenecks. Certain types of engineers and technicians may, for a time, be in short supply; but a large-scale, rapid diffusion of the robot may, indeed, pose an employment problem for the less skilled—a problem whose scale we cannot now measure.

I turn, therefore, to my fourth question, which I would re-phrase as follows: given the uncertain rate of expansion, employment, and skill requirements of the new innovational industries, the potential off-loading of unskilled workers into the labor market by robots, and the possible further loss of employment in older industries, is a return to full employment in the advanced industrial countries feasible?

Here we are dealing with very large issues, indeed; and in the compass of this short book I shall have to be both more cryptic and more dogmatic than I would wish.

Are the Older Manufacturing Industries Doomed?

The crossing of the curves of Japanese and U.S. steel and automobile production in recent years was, indeed, a dramatic event in the history of the world economy. But I do not believe that the older industries of the United States are doomed to disappear without trace to be supplanted by imports from Japan and from the emerging industrial countries of the developing world. In fact, I am extremely skeptical of the notion that we are entering a postindustrial society. The proportion of the working force in services has been rising for some time and it may continue to rise, but that does not mean that we are automatically destined to divest ourselves of the bulk of our manufacturing capacity.

I hold this view for the following reasons:

— Present low levels of output in those industries are the product not only of foreign competition but also of high interest rates and a deep domestic recession. After all, retail sales of new foreign-manufactured cars have been held by international agreement about constant in the period 1979–1982; but a drop of 29 percent occurred in domestic car sales. It is the decline in the overall demand rather than foreign imports which has mainly hurt the industry. The same is true for steel. The competitive position of both automobiles and steel was also badly hurt by the artificially high value of the dollar in 1981–1982, resulting from the abnormal interest rates imposed by monetary policy. Thus, a strong sustained, noninflationary revival of the economy as a whole would greatly ameliorate (but not wholly solve) the problem posed by the older basic industries.

— As for Japan, the American automobile industry could retrieve a part of the market lost, without corrosive protectionist devices, by the introduction of new technologies and management practices; and so could steel. Moreover, the relative rise of real wages in Japan is likely to mitigate part of its current comparative advantage if, working to a common purpose, American business and labor come to match Japanese technology and efficiency—a process not beyond their reach.

— As for the emerging industrial powers of the developing world, only a few are likely to command the domestic markets to generate efficient mass automobile and steel industries.

They can and should compete internationally. But, if those industries in the advanced industrial world take advantage of new, emerging technologies, they should remain viable at, probably, lower levels than their historical production peaks but much higher levels than at present when, for example, steel is operating at about 50 percent capacity.

This is the heart of the matter. The technologies of the Fourth Industrial Revolution exhibit great promise for the basic industries—for example, robots and new industrial materials. Indeed, if we do not maintain those industries, we shall not get the full benefit of those technologies. As we noted earlier, the hard-pressed automotive, electrical equipment, machinery, and fabricating metals industries are precisely the candidates for robots.

These older basic industries are not likely, of course, to resume the high growth rates of the 1950s and 1960s. Looking ahead, the decisive competitive battle in the advanced industrial world is likely to be over the technologies of the Fourth Industrial Revolution rather than the Third. But I do not believe the old basic industries are automatically headed for oblivion, if steady growth is resumed in the advanced industrial world, if entrepreneurship of a reasonably high order is exercised in those industries, including the application to them of some of the new technologies, and if labor cooperation in their transformation is achieved. This theme is pursued in chapter 6.

In fact, we require large basic industries as a foundation for national defense; and, if for no other reason, we had better set about rendering them efficient and competitive.

Thus, the technological rehabilitation of the older, basic industries should generate expanded flows of investment and employment in the boom of the 1980s and 1990s.

Investment Requirements for Basic Resources

Another major source of investment derives from what I have called the Fifth Kondratieff Upswing; and this I had better pause and explain.

A minor but persistent strand in the history of economic thought in the twentieth century is speculation about the possible existence of long cycles in the world economy. Such cycles are generally dated as 40 to 60 years in length. Over the two centuries of modern industrial growth now behind us, one cannot, therefore, find many cycles.

Although he had several predecessors, Nicolai Kondratieff, a Russian economist working in the 1920s, crystallized a body of evidence suggesting the reality of long cycles. His key data were prices, interest rates, and money wages. He found troughs around 1790, 1844–1851, and 1890–1896; peaks at 1810–1817, 1870–1875, and 1914–1920. He tried, but failed, to mobilize persuasive evidence that the two and a half long cycles he identified were reflected also in production data. And, in fact, he never developed, in his own phrase, "an appropriate theory of long waves." But he speculated in an interesting way about possible causes—for example, changes in technology, wars and revolutions, the bringing of new countries into the world economy, and fluctuations in gold production. Kondratieff's successors in this line of speculation have explored each of his leads. But, over the whole span since 1790, hypotheses about cycles in innovation, wars, gold discoveries, or cycles in overall growth rates break down when subjected to close analysis. The only hypothesis that does the job for the whole two-century era is one centered on the prices of basic commodities relative to manufactured products.

Specifically, I have taken the view that, with some foreshadowing in the second half of the 1960s, the world economy moved at the close of 1972 into the fifth protracted period of relatively high prices for basic commodities after experiencing some twenty years of absolute or relative decline in those commodities, starting in 1951. Thus, since 1951 we have lived, in my view, during the Fourth Kondratieff Downswing (when the relative prices of basic commodities fell) and a part, at least, of the Fifth Kondratieff Upswing.

I would underline that the cycles Kondratieff identified were by no means smooth sine curves. There are, even, elements of uniformity in their irregularity. Before 1914, for example, they began with a sharp, initial rise lasting a few years, after which the relative price of basic commodities oscillated in a high range. Of the trend rise in British prices in the First Kondratieff Upswing, 66 percent occurred between 1798 and

1801; in the second, 71 percent between 1852 and 1854; in the third, 57 percent between 1898 and 1900. The world economy experienced such a convulsive rise in 1973–1975, with subsequent oscillation in a high range (see chart 1B).

There was a second, fairly consistent irregularity. The upswings and downswings usually exhibited an interval or cycle in which the trend movement abated or reversed and, then, asserted itself again. In the British case, for example, the cycles of 1803–1808, 1832–1837, 1862–1868, 1886–1894, and 1904–1908 all, to a significant degree, ran against the trend. I shall raise the question later as to whether we are now experiencing such an interval.

For our purposes, however, the central phenomenon of a Kondratieff upswing is a shift in the direction of investment toward the expansion of supplies of (or substitutes for) the high-priced commodities in relatively short supply. On the downswing, with some interesting explicable exceptions, investment shifted toward industrial sectors, consumer goods, urban infrastructure, and service sectors where the relative profitability of investment was now favorable. That happened between 1951 and 1972.

As noted earlier, the Fifth Kondratieff Upswing began, at the close of 1972, with an explosion of grain prices, followed by a quadrupling of oil prices the next year. In both cases, exogenous events played a role—that is, the poor harvests of 1972–1973 and the Middle East War of October 1973. But, as noted earlier, a deeper examination makes clear that strong endogenous forces were at work in the late 1960s which decreed, in time, a reversal of post-1951 relative price trends.

Despite various government efforts to suppress or mitigate the impact of the energy price rise on consumers, the Kondratieff upswing process worked to a degree; that is, energy-related investment sharply increased. In the United States, for example, conventional energy investment rose from 1.8 percent of GNP in the mid 1960s to about 3.5 percent in 1981. This excludes large investments in energy conservation, which may have amounted to 3 percent of all capital outlays in 1981.

As of early 1983, of course, energy, food, and raw material prices were soft compared to their levels, say, two or three years earlier; and it is wholly fair to ask if the Fifth Kondratieff

Downswing has begun after a much shorter upswing than in the historical past. After all, the length of the upswings was often determined in the pre-1914 world by the time it took to open up new territories and bring them into large-scale, efficient production. Now much of the expansion will come from increases in productivity and the exploitation of already accessible resources. Moreover, the increase in energy prices was so extreme by historical standards that it might have induced more rapid compensatory adjustment than in the historical past.

On the other hand, it may well be that we have another transient break in the trend and the Fifth Kondratieff Upswing will reassert itself. Consider, for example, the following:
— In diminishing degree, geared to income elasticities of demand, the softening of raw materials, energy, and agricultural prices has been caused by the current severe recession. As of early 1983, the futures markets were already signaling a probable rise in the prices of industrial raw materials.
— Even then, near the bottom of the recession (September 1982), crude material prices (1967 = 100) in the United States stood at 317, total finished goods prices at 283. The real international price of oil, despite the recent decline, was still more than three times higher than in 1972 (see chart 8). The United States terms of trade, which had deterioriated relative to 1972 by 26 percent in the first quarter of 1980, were still 15 percent less favorable than they were a decade earlier in the second quarter of 1982 despite an artificially strong dollar (see chart 2). A revival in the world economy is likely to reverse, in some degree, the recent relative price shift in basic commodities and weaken the U.S. terms of trade.
— As for the future of the world oil price, no one's crystal ball is clear. In the short run, there are those, for example, who would argue that OPEC is about to self-destruct. They argue that OPEC will find it impossible to agree on sufficiently austere production quotas to sustain the present ($29 per barrel) posted price. A price war will follow. It could be brought about by progressive cheating on output and prices by OPEC members (for example, Iran) or price undercutting by other oil exporters (for example, the U.S.S.R., Mexico, Great Britain). Or, it could be brought about by a Saudi decision to teach some of the maverick

OPEC members that they had better hang together or they will hang separately—by expansion of Saudi production, which would drive the international oil price down to levels that most OPEC members could not bear. In both these dramatic scenarios, most analysts estimate $20 per barrel as a likely floor at which producers would be forced to come together to establish firm production quotas.

But the reader should be warned that, since 1973, the conventional wisdom has been notably unreliable in this field; and, as this is written (March 21, 1983), the oil futures market is betting that the $29 per barrel price will hold.

There is even less expert agreement on the long-run price of oil and energy. Some—probably a majority—argue that the real price of oil will resume its rise in the second half of the 1980s if the world economy generates a reasonably high and regular growth rate. In that case, a little-noted aspect of the pattern of world energy consumption is likely to reassert itself—namely, the much higher rates of increase in energy consumption in the developing regions than in the advanced industrial world. For example, primary energy consumption increased in the U.S. and Canada, between 1971 and 1981, at the rate of 0.8 percent per annum; in Western Europe at 1 percent; but in Latin America, the Middle East, Africa, and Asia at between 5.1 percent and 6.6 percent. History, in fact, is not linear; but primary energy consumption in the developing regions would exceed that in Western Europe and North America in a quarter-century, if the differential expansion rates of the 1970s were to persist. The reasons for the higher energy growth rates in the developing regions include higher real growth rates at this stage of their history than those of the advanced industrial countries; high rates of expansion of population in energy-intensive cities; the rapid absorption of energy-intensive technologies such as steel, metalworking, and chemicals; and high rates of expansion in motor vehicle use.

— There are some 21,000 oil fields in the world; but 2 percent of those fields hold 82 percent of the total recoverable oil, 5 percent hold 90 percent. Question marks hang over the probable future rates of production of certain great oil fields in the United States, the Soviet Union, and elsewhere; and the best geologists I know tell me it is unlikely that new finds, which will certainly be made, will match the run-down of existing established oil reserves. For example, depending on oil prices and drilling rates, oil production in Texas is likely to decline at 3–6 percent per annum over the next generation.

— Finally, the oil-producing region of the Middle East is not a particularly stable part of the world.

The implications for policy of both the short-run and the longer-run prospects for energy are explored in chapter 6.

With respect to agriculture, the inescapable increase of population in the developing regions, due to age structures, despite current declines in birthrates, may add something like 2 billion human beings to the planet in the next generation; and, overall, the rate of increase in agricultural production in those regions is not yet matching the rate of increase in the demand for food, inducing a rate of growth in grain imports of more than 3 percent per annum. In addition, there is the apparently intractable pathology of agriculture in most of the Communist states.

As for raw materials, there is evidence of underinvestment in recent years and distorted patterns of investment. In Latin America, for example, the tension between an understandable nationalist desire to control fully natural resources and an understandable desire of foreign investors for stable and reasonable terms for their outlays has resulted in a number of countries in reduced rates of raw material development. If the world economy revives, we may encounter raw material bottlenecks. Taking precisely this view of raw material prospects, the World Bank has estimated that 1977–2000 capital requirements for additional capacity in seven key minerals would come to $278 billion (in U.S. 1977 dollars), of which $96 billion constitutes investments in the developing countries. (In 1982 dollars the figures would be about $342 billion and $118 billion, respectively.)

Without dogmatism, I am inclined to believe, on balance, that the Fifth Kondratieff Upswing is not over if the world economy revives strongly in the 1980s.

For our purposes, this means that very large additional investments must take place within the world economy in energy, agriculture, and raw materials if growth is to go forward at normal rates and a still rapidly enlarging population accommodated with adequate food supplies.

There is another major form of resource-related investment that should be included in this array—that is, investment in rolling back degradation of the environment and maintaining for the long pull supplies of clean air and water, arable land, the forests, and irreplaceable areas for recreation and wildlife. These are tasks for both advanced industrial and developing countries. Over the past generation, the flow of investment for these purposes has greatly increased and there have been some notable areas of progress from, say, San Diego Bay and the Hudson River to the Chinese reforestation program. There are also many unsolved problems from, say, the pollution of water by chemicals from diffuse sources to the encroachment of the desert in central Africa. Systematic budgeting of investment for these purposes is clearly now an inescapable item on the national and international agenda.

We do not have the data required to estimate firmly the diversion of investment to these resource sectors required to maintain a viable world economy. Where calculations have been made, the numbers are large. For example, a World Bank estimate suggested that energy production investment requirements in the developing regions would approximate $683 billion (in 1980 U.S. dollars), with an annual investment growth rate of 12.3 percent, lifting the proportion of investment allocated to this purpose from 2.3 percent of GNP in 1980 to 3.2 percent in 1990. A good deal of this capital would have to come from abroad.

For Latin America alone, the Inter-American Development Bank estimated that in the course of the 1980s something on the order of $300 billion (in 1980 U.S. dollars) would be required for investment in energy production, about 45 percent of which would have to come from abroad. The proportion of GNP allocated to energy investment would, on these calculations, rise from something like 3 percent to 4.4 percent.

A recent study of the Asian Development Bank concludes that investment in energy production will have to double for the developing countries of Asia in 1980–1985 as compared to 1975–1980.

For the United States, my colleagues and I at the University of Texas estimated a few years ago that to render the United States a marginal net energy exporter, by full exploitation of coal and synthetics, would require a rise in the proportion of energy production investment to GNP from 3.5 percent to at least 4.2 percent.

As in the other Kondratieff upswings, part of the increased investment in resources will occur in the relatively advanced industrial countries, depending on their resource endowments, and part in what we call developing regions. Depending on how North-South relations evolve or are organized, a substantial expansion of employment opportunities should emerge in industries, both old and new, in the advanced industrial countries.

Thus, the possibility and need exist for a new North-South partnership centered on the key resource sectors requiring expanded investment; and that partnership could generate greatly expanded employment in northern export industries as well as capital movements from North to South. We shall return to this point in chapter 6.

If, by appropriate investment patterns and the introduction of new technologies, the world economy succeeds in inducing the Fifth Kondratieff Downswing over, say, the next decade, the consequent sustained relative decline of basic commodity prices and improved terms of trade would, of course, accelerate the rise of real incomes in the advanced industrial countries and ease the pressures on the manufacturing sectors and urban areas of developing countries. The world economy would return, in a sense, to the pattern of the 1950s and 1960s. The income elasticity of demand (that is, consumers' preferences as incomes expand) might express itself in somewhat different ways than it then did. But thus far, at least, our peoples have not experienced difficulty in finding ways to spend higher real incomes, although the proportion of income saved might rise.

Investment Requirements for Infrastructure

Now, another source of additional employment of a kind capable of engaging unskilled as well as skilled labor, that is, the backlog of investment which has developed in basic infrastructure—roads, highways, bridges, water supply, sewerage, pollution control, and so on. I have already suggested the forces which have yielded this backlog. It has been well dramatized in the media, and limited action has been taken by the Congress with respect to road repair financed by a gasoline tax. The backlog is estimated at anywhere from $650 billion to $2.5 trillion (1982) if previous infrastructure standards are to be reattained. (The range is explained, in part, by the fact that the larger figure includes items for ports and inland waterways, prison facilities, and water pollution control not included in the smaller.) Even for a $3 trillion economy, and even if spread out over ten or fifteen years, this is a formidable increment of required investment with large implications for employment prospects over a wide range of skills. Total fixed nonresidential investment in 1982 was $347 billion. Taking the lower estimate of infrastructure requirements ($650 billion) and a fifteen-year interval to meet them, a 12 percent annual increase in the 1982 overall investment figure is implied. The higher figure ($25 trillion) implies a rather unlikely 48 percent increase in the 1982 investment figure.

Taken all together, the potentialities of the Fourth Industrial Revolution, the need to modernize the older industries, the imperatives of the Fifth Kondratieff Upswing and the enlarged exports to the developing regions they should generate, and the investments required to make good the infrastructure backlog decree that authentic investment requirements of the United States are high. If exploited by a return to low real interest rates and appropriate public policies, they should provide ample employment opportunities over the foreseeable future for the U.S. working force, skilled and unskilled.

Thus, while the leading sectors of the boom of the 1980s and 1990s are, as I suggested at the beginning, quite different from those of the 1950s and 1960s, there is no question that the investment requirements exist for a powerful sustained economic expansion in the United States and the world economy.

Inflation: The Lion in the Path

Now the critical question, for, evidently, a lion stands in our path—our incapacity to reconcile high growth rates with effective control over inflation. If we go on as we have since 1973, with stop-and-go policies and low average growth rates, low investment rates, and much idle capacity, the diffusion of the new technologies will be slowed, among other things, by the resistance of the unions. The decline of the old basic industries will continue. The will to deal creatively with the developing regions will be feeble. The erosion of America's physical and social infrastructure will be progressive. High levels of unemployment will, indeed, then become chronic. To avoid this outcome, we shall, evidently, have to find ways to control inflation by means other than monetary restraint, high real interest rates, and the discipline of chronic unemployment, idle capacity, and low investment rates they impose. As of early 1983, it is clearly the fear of revived rising inflation rates that is leading the Reagan administration to project extremely low growth and continued high unemployment (9–10 percent) for the year ahead; and, in addition to the large federal deficit, it is a lack of faith that prices can be restrained in the context of a revived economy that helps keep real interest rates high in the capital markets.

For three years we tried to walk the line between high growth and inflation by control over the rate of growth in the money supply. The experiment yielded the deepest recession since the 1930s, a grotesque federal deficit, and, despite a subsidence of inflation, continued high real interest rates. Now some, at least, are trying to evoke fiscal policy (reduced expenditures and higher taxes) to narrow the deficit and bring down real interest rates. We have tried successively to sit on one-legged stools: first, monetary policy, now fiscal policy. In fact, we need a three-legged stool. Without the third leg, monetary and fiscal policy are being asked to do more than they can accomplish either singly or together.

The critical third leg is what is called among economists an incomes policy—that is, a method for gearing average wage and salary increases to the average rate of productivity increase, thus eliminating the core rate of inflation. With a firm incomes policy, the instruments of macroeconomic policy can play the balancing role they are capable of performing.

I shall have a good deal more to say about incomes policies in chapter 6. I would only make a few general observations here.

First, given our experiences since the close of 1972, only an effective incomes policy, supplemented by appropriate fiscal and monetary policy, is likely to bring real interest rates down to their normal 1.5 – 3 percent level and keep them down. An incomes policy is thus needed to unleash the pent-up forces which would otherwise yield a powerful surge of investment in many directions.

Second, the creation and maintenance of an effective incomes policy transcend conventional economic policy. It is a problem of generating and institutionalizing a working consensus on a critical issue in societies otherwise dedicated to vigorous competitive contention. It is, essentially, a constitutional problem and should be approached as such with appropriate gravity. In democratic societies, we maintain minimum order amidst competitive contention by accepting a framework of agreed constitutional rules which the overwhelming majority of the people judge to be fair. Incomes policies must now be added to those rules.

The history of the years since 1945 is littered with failed efforts by democratic societies to sustain incomes policies. There have been periods of success for a good many countries; and four have sustained them quite well over a longer span: Japan, Austria, the Federal Republic of Germany, and Switzerland. But the second most important point to be made about incomes policies is that they are difficult and pose deep-seated political and institutional problems. If they were easy to install and maintain they would long since have been in operation everywhere.

The most important thing to be said about incomes policies, however, is that, whatever the difficulties, we shall have to overcome them if we are to sustain viable and civilized societies in the present and foreseeable environment of the world economy.

What is required politically is the bringing together of our societies around a palpable, fully shared, overriding long-run interest—an interest in sustained noninflationary growth—at the cost of abandoning chimerical short-run interests and zero-sum game attitudes.

Institutionally, an incomes policy requires that we install arrangements for annual wage bargaining at the national level, where the common requirement of avoiding inflation is there on the table, to replace the fragmented sectoral wage negotiations that have emerged out of our history. In such negotiations the rate of inflation is taken essentially as an exogenous variable, beyond the negotiators' control or responsibility. Out of our history we have inherited a system of industry-by-industry negotiations conducted at different times, usually yielding multiyear contracts. The importance of these institutional facts in maintaining the momentum of inflation is universally recognized. For example, both the final (1981) *Economic Report of the President to the Congress* of the Carter administration and the first (1982) *Economic Report* of the Reagan administration discussed the inflationary role of these institutional procedures. But neither proposed a remedy.

Our present collective bargaining arrangements, which frustrate an expression of the common interest, did not come down from a mountain in marble like the Ten Commandments. They are not written into the Constitution. They are not governed by the rules of free competitive markets. They are quasimonopolistic negotiations which emerged from a complex political and social history, reaching back a half-century, if one takes the NRA as a bench mark, a century if one starts with the origins of a serious labor union movement in the United States, organized on an industry-by-industry basis. The simple fact is that the negotiation of wages, industry by industry, at different times, often covering periods of up to three years, no longer serves the nation's interest or labor's. We need a system which automatically brings into play the common interest in avoiding inflation, an interest screened out by the system history has given us.

A national wage norm cannot, of course, be universally applied. There must be a range of flexibility in money wage increases to permit rapidly growing, high-productivity industries to draw labor while others (as, indeed, at present) increase real wages at less than the average rate of productivity increase. Each country will have to work out these arrangements in terms of its own history, circumstances, and inherited institutions. But we know two exceedingly important things from the relatively successful cases: incomes policies need not impose undue rigidities on the working of markets or otherwise prevent vital private sectors from operating; they can be designed so that they are judged to be fair by both business and labor.

Obviously, judgments on the capacity of our societies to make such institutional changes and sustain them will differ; and there is room for legitimate debate. I would only say here— and argue further in chapter 6—that, under strong presidential leadership, I believe the United States, as a society, is now capable of mounting and sustaining such arrangements once the stakes involved are fully and well explained.

Three Additional Tasks for Public Policy

There are policy implications of this call for a civilized synthesis that transcend the fundamental question of reconciling control over inflation with regular growth. I would cite three, all of which require a significant change in attitude among some of the leaders of the counter-revolution we have been experiencing on both sides of the Atlantic. One of the banners of the counter-revolution, at its extreme, is that governments can do no economic good. I, for one, am prepared to argue that, in some directions, government actions have been excessive; a weighing of costs and benefits is appropriate, as is a pruning out. I would also argue that government should not intrude if the private sector can do the job. But, against the background of firmly installed incomes policies and the character of the probable leading sectors in the boom envisaged here for the 1980s and 1990s, there are legitimate tasks to be performed which only governments can perform. For example:

— Tax and other government initiatives could accelerate the diffusion of the Fourth Industrial Revolution, including a limited government role in retraining those components of the working force displaced by the new technologies.

— Under conditions specified in chapter 6 there is a legitimate role for the public sector in the rehabilitation of the older basic industries.

— Government policies and negotiations are required to set an appropriate framework for a North-South partnership of the kind I have suggested, although a substantial part of the increased capital flows to the South could be private.

— The rehabilitation of infrastructure is, evidently, a task primarily for public authorities.

In short, while certain functions of government may require reduction or constraint, others may require expansion, notably those directed toward the stimulus of investment in appropriate directions—for, initially at least, the potential boom of the 1980s and 1990s would be driven by expanded investment rather than by expanding real incomes lifted by favorable terms of trade. Real incomes would certainly rise with the increase in employment and productivity a sustained boom would yield. But the primary engine at work in the process would be expanded private investment, encouraged at the margin with supportive public policies, plus enlarged public investment in infrastructure. It is, therefore, time for a more discriminating view of the appropriate relation between the public and private sectors.

A Civilized Synthesis?

I have called the policy outlined here a civilized synthesis and the reader deserves to know why. I believe it is civilized because, if it is rightly conceived and effectively executed, it would provide for the United States high levels of employment, control over inflation, decent social services, the rebuilding of our rapidly obsolescing industrial plant and physical infrastructure, and sufficient command over the new technologies to assure for the United States a strong, competitive position in the world economy over the decades ahead. Without doing these things, the American economy, essentially living off its accumulated but waning capital base, will deteriorate progressively and experience the kind of vicious conflict that is generated when people fight for shares in a diminishing pie. Declining societies are not very attractive.

The approach is a synthesis because it would accept part of the counter-revolution, reject part, and add new elements. In controlling inflation, it would, of course, allow a role for monetary policy; but it would insist that inflation can be controlled only by combining monetary and fiscal policy with a serious long-term incomes policy. It would accept the need to prune and discipline the rate of rise of transfer payments; but it would not pursue the cutback of those expenditures as an overriding goal of public policy at the bottom of a deep recession. It would accept the need for the maximum use of private markets and of fiscal and administrative measures to encourage the vitality of the private sector; but it would insist that there are major, inescapable public responsibilities with respect to the economy, some of them new responsibilities.

Above all, the nature of the tasks before us decrees a coming together of all the major groups in our society to achieve common civic purposes. That is the ultimate civilized synthesis the argument of this book implies.

So much for the conceptual basis for a new economic policy. I turn now to describe some of the lines of action required to bring it to life, for a judgment on its viability requires somewhat more detail than this chapter has provided.

6. What Is to Be Done?

When presented with a new idea, President Kennedy would typically ask: "What do you want me to do about it today?" President Johnson would simply lean forward and say: "Therefore?" In that spirit, this chapter is an effort to render more concrete and operational the broad approach to national and international economic policy outlined in chapter 5.

The package of commended policies that flow from chapter 5 can be grouped under five headings as follows:

A. Installing a Long-Term Policy for the Control of Inflation
B. Nurturing the Fourth Industrial Revolution
C. Rehabilitating the Older Basic Industries
D. Coping with the Fifth Kondratieff Upswing
E. Rebuilding the Nation's Infrastructure

The central argument is quite simple. An effective long-term policy for the control of inflation would bring real interest rates down to their natural low level, in the range of 1–3 percent, and keep them there. Low real interest rates would, in themselves, unleash a large increase in long-term investment as well as greatly expanded sales of houses, automobiles, and durable consumer goods. A strong business expansion would begin in the private sector. But the structure—the investment pattern—of the boom of the 1980s and 1990s should differ greatly from that of the 1950s and 1960s. To assure that certain structural problems of the national and international economy were dealt with, supplementary public policies would be required. They are of a character that would reinforce—not usurp, intrude upon, or damp—the actions of the private sector.

A. *Installing a Long-Term Policy for the Control of Inflation*

The view taken in this book is that the long-term control of inflation requires the combined use of fiscal, monetary, and incomes policies. In addition, as comments made thus far on energy, medical costs, and productivity suggest, it requires efforts to minimize the price rise in particular sectors, as well as actions over a wide front to reduce core inflation by generating a high, steady rate of productivity increase.

I shall begin with incomes policy because it is the most controversial component in the recommended long-term inflation control program. In fact, there is virtually a conspiracy of silence among American politicians of both parties on this point, although many are well aware of the option.

If one reviews the methods of various countries to bring about a gearing of wage to productivity increases, one finds a considerable range of procedures and institutional devices. The technical common characteristics are the enunciation (or negotiation) of an explicit or implicit wage norm in terms of national rather than industry-by-industry criteria; the provision of a forum in which business and labor exchange views and negotiate in terms of such national criteria; the provision of some wage flexibility as between rapidly growing, high-productivity industries and less dynamic sectors; the conduct of supplementary fiscal, monetary, and other policies that are required to make the wage settlements realistic, equitable, and, thus, acceptable. Perhaps most important of all, wage contracts are set annually and, usually, at roughly the same period. Spring seems to be a preferred season.

Take, for example, Japan's wage-setting system. It is based on four elements, none of which is inscrutably oriental. Indeed, it was adapted in the mid 1950s from prior Western efforts in this field.

1. Every spring, business, major labor unions, and the government negotiate to establish a norm for wage increases. The norm is based on all the key factors affecting the national economy: the expected rate of increase in productivity, the balance of payments position, unemployment, and so on. The norm

does not hold for all wage increases: flexibility is allowed for more or less dynamic industries and firms within them, as in any system of wage guideposts. About a quarter of the labor force is directly affected by the spring negotiation, but it has a much wider influence on wage setting throughout the economy.

2. During the year, regular meetings are held by business and labor and government officials to review the economy's position and problems. These are not negotiating sessions; but, when spring negotiations arrive, there is a common, realistic view of the scope for noninflationary wage increases. Spring bargaining is over a narrow range.

3. Part of the workers' income takes the form of a semi-annual bonus primarily geared to each firm's profits—a useful and theoretically correct way for providing deviations from the national wage norm.

4. Against the background of wage payments linked to the average rate of increase in productivity, fiscal and monetary policy are freed to do jobs they can do: they help the economy avoid overheating, and they stimulate the economy when unemployment rises.

Three special features of Japan's method should be noted: direct price controls are used selectively to damp the inflation rate and inflationary expectations, notably those set or influenced by public authorities; monetary policy is not conducted wholly in aggregate terms but targeted to achieve special policy objectives in particular sectors; the Japanese union structure is firm-oriented rather than industry-oriented.

In Germany and Austria, on the other hand, understandings about appropriate wage increases are arrived at among strong, highly centralized industrial and labor groups. In Germany, the annual contract with the metalworkers' union is generally negotiated first and tends to set the national pattern which is firmed up by other negotiations in the spring. A council of five experts provides an analysis of the economy's prospects and, in effect, sets the framework for wage negotiations. Both Germany and Austria provide institutional arrangements for sustained labor-management discourse on the prospects for the economy as a whole independent of the wage-negotiating process. The Austrian arrangements, as one would expect in a very small, homogeneous country, are even more centralized than the German.

Australia, out of a long history, developed state and federal conciliation and arbitration commissions which play a central role in wage determination, with the Federal Commission taking precedence in case of a conflict in rulings.

In all cases, the role of international influence on domestic prices has complicated the national task, a subject to which we shall return.

The institutional arrangements devised by each country evidently reflect their special circumstances, including the union structures which have evolved out of their several histories. But, in the end, as Austrian Finance Minister Hans Seidel told the Joint Economic Committee of the Congress on June 2, 1981, their success depended on an acceptance, as far as the reconciliation of growth and control over inflation are concerned, of a social partnership. "Social partnership," Seidel said, "does not just mean that we all sit in the same boat. It also means that we are willing to steer the boat in a direction upon which most of us agree." This requires, of course, a sense of equity in the outcome.

In the United States we accepted price and wage controls during the Second World War and the Korean War; and virtually every post-1945 administration has been driven, against its will, to make some kind of direct approach to inducing wage and price restraint. The story of these efforts down to the Nixon administration is chronicled in *Exhortation and Controls*, edited by Craufurd Goodwin. In his January 25, 1983, State of the Union message, even Reagan took an important step on what might prove a salutary slippery slope by urging a wage freeze in the federal government.

What we have never done in the United States is to pause and ask ourselves this question: how could we organize our affairs and institutions in such a way as to provide over the long term a system in which average wage increases were geared to the average rate of productivity increase in a way that was consistent with a vital private sector and judged equitable by labor?

Kennedy's initiatives of 1961–1962 were quite successful but did not meet this test. At the bottom of the recession which existed when he came to responsibility, Kennedy negotiated an ad hoc deal by exploiting the back-to-back auto and steel wage negotiations which happened to come up in 1961 and 1962. At that time these two industries tended to set the wage increase pattern for much of the economy. The deal, made in the summer of 1961, was as follows: Walter Reuther (automobiles) accepted a 2½ percent money wage increase on two conditions: David McDonald (steel) would get only 2½ percent, and there would be no rise in the steel price. The average rate of productivity increase was then calculated at 2½ percent, and the situation in the steel industry approximated this average. As Reuther predicted, the steel industry announced a steel price rise in the wake of McDonald's settlement at 2½ percent; and a noisy seventy-two-hour battle ensued in April 1962 before the steel price increase was rescinded. The enunciation of formal wage-price guideposts in the 1962 *Economic Report of the President to the Congress* can be understood only in the context of the Kennedy-Reuther deal.

The upshot was quite impressive. Kennedy's policy yielded an average annual increase in the consumer price index for the period 1961–1965 of 1.3 percent as opposed to 3.6 percent for the U.K.; 3.6 percent for the Netherlands; 3.7 percent for Sweden; 3.8 percent for France; and 2.8 percent for Germany. This relative performance strengthened the U.S. balance of payments position within the constraints of the Bretton Woods system and provided the breathing room to expand the domestic economy and enlarge foreign aid by about 30 percent. But Kennedy's ad hoc deal was never explained to the people with the full weight its importance justified, and the subsequent wage-price guideposts lacked both a legal and an institutional basis.

Johnson carried forward the wage-price guidepost policy. But without a firm political, legal, and institutional foundation, it cracked with the airline machinists' strike and its settlement in the summer of 1966—in my judgment, a quite unnecessary failure. But the basic point is that the whole system was infirmly based. It was explicitly abandoned by Nixon on

January 27, 1969, unleashing a phase of stagflation and balance of payments deterioration which led him by August 15, 1971, to install wage-price controls.

There is not much point, at this critical juncture in our history, to allocating praise or blame for past efforts at disciplining inflation in American society. But it is useful to examine the efforts of the United States and others to grapple with what is evidently one of the greatest challenges democratic societies have ever faced. Indeed, my first recommendation is that the executive branch and the Congress conduct a systematic review of the success stories, partial success stories, and failures in trying to make incomes policies work. The Joint Economic Committee has gone some distance in this direction, but a lack of consensus among its members has prevented it from coming to grips seriously with how incomes policies might be organized in the United States.

Assume for a moment that my analysis is correct and that we require a long-term incomes policy (along with other, more familiar antiinflationary measures) to get real interest rates down, keep them down, and thus release the forces for sustained growth we have thus far skillfully managed to repress. How might we proceed?

We are talking about a major change in the nation's institutional arrangements, affecting all the people, requiring the participation of all the relevant groups in the society. It demands substantial consensus and a sense of equity. We must begin, therefore, with the president. Having decided this course was essential for the general welfare he has sworn to uphold, he would have to build a consensus with the bipartisan leadership of the Congress, business, labor, and citizen groups and go to the country in a strong, unambiguous way. There is no point making such an effort unless it is done with a total commitment by the president to see it through. To recall Theodore Roosevelt's characterization of the German chancellor in 1914, this is no business for a president who "means well feebly." The optimum time would be early in a new administration. Carter in 1977 and Reagan in 1981 had such opportunities. But Reagan, like Nixon, may be forced in this direction by the course of events in 1983–1984. If he were to throw himself into the effort with, say, as much energy as he expended in achieving the 1981 tax cut, he could be extremely effective.

In any case, every knowledgeable economic analysis of which I am aware concludes on a noneconomic note: the mobilization of a political consensus around the simple proposition that it is an overriding common national interest to achieve regular growth, low unemployment, with inflation under firm control, is fundamental to the success of an incomes policy. And I am deeply convinced that, after our experiences of the past two decades, such a consensus is latent in American public opinion and among a substantial majority of businessmen, labor leaders, and the Congress. But only a determined president can evoke and render effective that consensus.

There is a technical point here which should be brought into the open. It is often argued that a discussion by responsible public officials of incomes policies is dangerous. The expectation of possible wage-price limitations will lead business and labor to anticipate that possibility by raising wages and prices immediately so that they would be in a more advantageous position when the incomes policy is installed. A rollback provision in legislation to implement an incomes policy could deal with the problem; and it may, in any case, be necessary. But the problem could be minimized if the president, after private consultation with the bipartisan leadership, should ask privately for the prompt reenactment of the 1970 amendment to the Defense Production Act of 1950. That amendment granted to the president wage- and price-setting powers. I would guess that it would be granted quite promptly by the Congress. It could contain a rollback provision.

Immediately upon its enactment, three actions might be set in motion:

— A major address to, say, a joint session of the Congress outlining the president's strategy and the case for it.

— The convening of a business-labor-citizen group (including a few senior members of Congress from both parties) to thrash out the legislative basis, institutional shape, and procedures for a long-run incomes policy which would meet the criteria of minimum intrusion on the private sector, equity, and effectiveness. This group would have a major public figure as chairman,

of known stubborn determination, and a small, first-class sec-
retariat. The group (subsequently, EOB Committee) should be
locked up in the Executive Office Building across from the
White House with the understanding that it would be at it full-
time and steadily until an agreement was reached.

— The imposition of a temporary wage-salary-dividends
freeze while the committee deliberated. Agricultural and raw
material prices would not be frozen, since their international
character renders national control measures ineffective and
often counterproductive. There might be occasion to monitor
prices in certain key quasimonopolistic industries to assure
that the occasion is not seized to shift income from wages to
profits, although the dividends freeze would deal with the most
corrosive aspect of the problem because the plowback of profits
into investment in a firm's capital stock is of fundamental importance for labor's productivity and real wage as well as for
future profits.

The freeze, which would hold until a long-term incomes
policy system was agreed, would serve the dual function of preventing anticipatory price and wage increases, as the incomes
policy system was being devised, and, even more important,
eliminating core inflation from the economic system at a
stroke, thus permitting the follow-on incomes policy arrangements to start from scratch.

On the other hand, a freeze should be as short as the pub-
lic-spiritedness of the members of the EOB Committee, the
toughness and negotiating skill of its chair, and the external
pressure of public opinion, generated by the president's continued exposition of his policy, can achieve. Ninety days might
be about right. Freezes become awkward with the passage of
time, preventing necessary shifts in relative wages and, thus,
prices.

What might the EOB Committee devise? On this matter I
would not attempt to be precise. One should defer to Jean
Monnet's dictum about his planning to modernize the French
economy launched in 1946: "I am sure of one thing. One cannot transform the French economy without the people par-
ticipating in the transformation. When I say the people, it is
not an abstract entity. I am referring to the unions, business
firms, government departments, and all those who will be as-

sociated with the plan." This would certainly hold for a transformation of wage negotiation procedures in this complex continental society.

The essential elements on the agenda of the EOB Committee would, evidently, be these:

1. A general criterion for average national wage (and salary)
increases and criteria for deviations from the average.

2. A time and procedure for negotiating an average wage
increase norm and a single concentrated interval for annual industry negotiations within its framework.

3. Machinery for regular business, labor, and government
consultation, throughout the year, without negotiation, on the
state of the national economy focused on variables which bear
on the scope for noninflationary wage increases (productivity,
unemployment, external inflationary pressures, balance of
payments, price changes, and so on).

4. Criteria for maintaining approximately constant shares
of labor and capital in the national income (as, for example, in
the case of Austria) or business-labor agreement on an increase
in the proportion of income invested, which may well be possible given labor's awareness of the need to rehabilitate old basic
industries, increase infrastructure investment, and generally
raise the amount of capital per worker, which has declined in
the United States at serious cost to productivity and real wages.

5. A procedure for monitoring prices in quasimonopolistic
industries to assure that the criteria agreed under 1 and 4,
above, are carried out.

6. Recommendations for whatever legal and legislative
basis for the arrangement may be agreed. This would include
examination of whether some form of tax-based incomes policy (TIP), using carrot, stick, or both, would be helpful as a supplementary device.

The EOB group should also examine the pros and cons of
recommending a version of the Japanese system of bonuses
to the working force, depending on a firm's profits; and it
should come firmly to grips with the problem of COLA's in both
the public and the private sectors. The automatic adjustment of
wages to cost-of-living increases in no way guarantees the level
of real wages (or other forms of income). These adjustments
simply perpetuate the inflationary process and, by providing an

illusion that real incomes are being protected, weaken the will to control inflation.

Standing back from this array of matters to be agreed by the EOB Committee (and then the president and the Congress), two observations are worth making which may relieve the sense that some such system would put the economy in a straitjacket. First, it should be recalled that what is proposed is not a detailed wage-price control system of the sort we have applied in wartime circumstances or in the first phase of Nixon's 1971–1972 arrangements. Much of our economy is competitive, and it would automatically respond, through market mechanisms, to the wage settlement patterns set in certain key industries and the public sector. Arrangements of this kind have proved thoroughly compatible with vital, flexible, private sectors in a number of countries, including those which have proved most successful in sustaining incomes policies, for example, Japan, Austria, Switzerland, and Germany.

Second, in one sense what is proposed is the more systematic application for the short term of something like Nixon's wage-price freeze of 1971, to be followed as soon as possible by a more orderly and formal version of Kennedy's guideposts of 1962. Both provided a setting for intervals of important improvement in the nation's economic performance and did no serious damage to the private sector. On the contrary.

Nonetheless, important changes are implicit in the proposals—namely, the way labor unions (and labor leaders) look at their role in the society and businessmen look at their price decisions. By the nature of the proposed institutional changes, business and labor would be required to negotiate in terms of their long-run interests. Every businessman knows that inflation leads to stop-and-go policies, that profits are exceedingly volatile, and that they plummet in recessions. They understand well that a policy to maximize profits over a reasonably long period of time should be noninflationary. Similarly, labor leaders know that, even if wage settlements manage to keep up with the cost of living under inflationary conditions, which has not been the case over the past decade, the real income of labor will suffer over a reasonably long period of time from the higher average unemployment and reduced rates of investment and productivity increase that are brought about by stop-and-go policies.

At the present time, the heart of the bargain with labor would be rules of wage restraint accepted in return for an expansionary monetary policy. Every central banker in advanced industrial countries, including Paul Volcker, would acknowledge that an effective incomes policy and the prospects for narrowing the budgetary deficit rapid economic expansion would provide would permit him in good conscience to join in that bargain.

Put another way, business-labor collective bargaining would by no means end under an effective incomes policy. What would end would be wage negotiations, oriented simply to the situation at a moment in time in a given industry, which take the rate of inflation as independent of the outcome of that negotiation and thereby build inflation into that sector for two or three years. In effect, an incomes policy permits business and labor negotiators to reflect their own long-run interests while still leaving them plenty to negotiate about at the margin.

This is not a trivial change. But, given the pass at which we have arrived, it ought to be possible. If the effort fails, we would not be the first society to prefer to go down in the style to which it had become accustomed rather than to face reality. The reality of the past quarter-century is that uncontrolled inflation has forced a series of recessions costly to employment, productivity, profit, real wages, our balance of payments, and the nation's social and physical infrastructure.

One final point of personal judgment about incomes policies. What I have had to say thus far about incomes policies has assumed that the correct general criterion is an average rate of money wage increase equal to the average rate of productivity increase.

I would, in fact, prefer an alternative formula: average fixed money wages with prices falling with the rate of increase of productivity. I am quite aware of the objections to this formula, notably the rising real burden of debts fixed in money terms, although this would be countered by low interest rates. I would opt for this formula for the following reasons.

— Passing along productivity increases in lower prices would greatly reduce the likelihood of public service (and other) strikes, which are peculiarly disruptive in an era where a quite substantial proportion of the working force is in the public service.

— The formula would make it easier to focus the attention of the society on the rate of productivity increase as the only basis for rising real incomes per worker.

— In particular, as in the periods 1815–1848 and 1873–1876, when falling price trends prevailed, such a formula would exert strong pressure on technologically sluggish firms to modernize or see their profit margins attenuated.

Labor leaders knowledgeable in economic history are quite aware that, as far as the real wages of labor are concerned, the optimum setting is one of stable money wages and falling prices.

I would not argue my criterion as a decisive issue; but its advantages and disadvantages, compared with those of the more conventional criterion, should be considered.

As I have tried to make clear, there is much more to a stable long-run policy to control inflation than an effective incomes policy.

On the demand side, a coordinated fiscal and monetary policy is required to avoid the emergence of demand-pull inflation. Since about two-thirds of the present federal deficit is the product of the recession itself, a return to steady high-growth rates would bring down that deficit and permit a flexibility in fiscal policy now denied us. But full employment and the emergence of bottlenecks would not occur in our great economy simultaneously. There is, therefore, a good case for the Federal Reserve to be prepared to operate selectively by sectors and regions along the general lines of the Japanese method.

On the supply side, the battle against inflation must also be fought sectorally, by antimonopoly policies, including liberal international trade policies, measures to constrain price increases in particular sectors (for example, medical services), and by policies to increase raw materials supply, including, in some cases, the building of stockpiles to cope with periods of raw materials-push inflation. Given the peculiar importance of the gyrations in energy prices since 1973 in determining the course of the world economy, and the long lead times of major forms of energy investment, a steady, long-run U.S. energy policy is required, the character of which is suggested in section D, below.

Recalling that core inflation is defined by the gap between money wage and productivity increases, a broad-based policy to accelerate the increase of productivity and to diffuse the Fourth Industrial Revolution to all relevant sectors evidently has a central place in a policy to control inflation. Certain particular observations on this problem are included in sections B and C, below. The most important general observation to be made on this point is that the maintenance of a steady high rate of noninflationary growth is the optimum environment for encouraging both large private sector R&D outlays and the rapid incorporation into the capital stock of new technologies. In a world of rapidly changing technology, investment to replace obsolescent equipment automatically incorporates more productive capital equipment.

An effective incomes policy would have an additional consequence for the behavior of the working force. Once it is clear and accepted that real wages can be raised in a sustainable way only by productivity increases and that an incomes policy will permit a rapid decrease in unemployment, it might well be possible to elicit sustained support from labor for efforts and new measures to enlarge investment and to introduce new technologies.

The central point is, simply, that the control over inflation—even with an effective incomes policy—requires unremitting supplementary efforts on both the demand and the supply sides of the equation.

B. *Nurturing the Fourth Industrial Revolution*

The character of the technologies embraced in what I have called the Fourth Industrial Revolution makes it possible for a high proportion of the relevant R&D to be carried forward by the private sector. Assuming that we can create an environment of low real interest rates—and the expectation of continued low real interest rates—and assuming that control over inflation permits high and reasonably steady growth in the private sector, we can expect innovation to proceed rapidly, by normal market processes, in exploitation of the microchip in all its ramified applications, new communications methods, the insights of genetics, the robot and laser, and new industrial materials.

There are, nevertheless, three broad areas where the possibility or need exists for public policies to support or accelerate invention and rapid diffusion of the new technologies. There is an important supplementary role for public R&D; a wide-ranging set of tasks in academic research, education, and the training and retraining of the work force; and the need for a substantial public role in certain kinds of investment which would accelerate the diffusion and otherwise support the whole complex process involved in the Fourth Industrial Revolution.

The new technologies differ from some of their great predecessors (for example, the steam engine, iron manufacture from coke, factory-manufactured cotton textiles, the railroads, steel, the internal-combustion engine) in a particular respect. Once the initial breakthroughs were made in most of the older revolutionary innovations, progressive refinements in their efficiency could take place pragmatically, on the job, in the private sector. Those refinements were of immense importance in cutting costs in the leading sectors of their time. But, in general, the process did not require extensive basic research and experimental pilot projects. Conversely, certain of the contemporary revolutionary innovations (like the electricity, chemical, and aerospace industries in the past) are linked to scientific fields where basic knowledge is still rapidly expanding, for example, genetics. That is why we have seen in a number of regions of the country new, vital linkages growing up between the research universities and the private sector. The 1980s are clearly a time for expanded public R&D in support of the fast-moving basic sciences underpinning the Fourth Industrial Revolution.

There is another limited, possible role for public policy. The spectrum running from basic science to invention to commercial application is complex. It can involve many more stages than this oversimplified tripartite breakdown suggests. Quite often a promising invention requires a pilot project of considerable cost and risk to establish whether a cost-effective innovation is likely to emerge. Fusion is an extreme but clear example of this requirement. In some cases, large firms in the private sector are prepared and are in a position to accept the cost and risk of this kind of substantial development outlay. But a good many dimensions of the Fourth Industrial Revolution are being carried forward by small or medium-size firms. Therefore, it would be wholly appropriate for the government to help finance promising but expensive and uncertain pilot projects in the development stage that are unlikely to be undertaken by the private sector. Similarly, it would be appropriate for the government to provide certain key research universities with funds to purchase the most advanced computers, now mainly restricted to military use in the U.S. but not in Japan and Western Europe.

There is, in addition, one sector in which public R&D has historically played a dominant role because the production units were too small to do the the the job—that is, agriculture. The shift in the structure of agriculture toward larger units and the emergence of R&D outlays by private firms in the food, fiber, and forestry industries have, to a degree, altered the initial almost monopolistic role of public sector R&D. Nevertheless, its role remains extremely important, notably in the land grant colleges. As the marginal productivity of existing agricultural technologies inevitably decelerates with the passage of time, new technologies must be developed and diffused. The application of genetics to agriculture appears particularly promising and, indeed, is already beginning to yield practical results. The fostering of this linkage and other potentialities for new agricultural technologies belongs on the agenda of public policy.

A second role for public policy in the Fourth Industrial Revolution lies, evidently, in the field of education: from the primary schools to the graduate schools and faculty research. It was wholesome that this role was, to a degree, recognized in Reagan's State of the Union message of January 25, 1983, as well as in the film incorporating the Democratic view of the State of the Nation broadcast that evening. The issues are now before the public and increasingly familiar: from the weaknesses in elementary school training in mathematics and science to the shortage of graduate scientists and engineers and the obsolescence of university laboratories. A protracted and stubborn effort at local, state, and national levels to invest more in education and to alter its balance will be required to provide the fundamental underpinnings for a successful diffusion and management of the Fourth Industrial Revolution.

The linkage between the existence of first-class concentrations of academic research and the presence of high-tech industries is palpable, although a number of other factors appear also to affect plant location. The presence of clusters of research universities clearly helps account for the extraordinary R&D concentrations in California and Massachusetts. A wholesome process of diffusion is now taking place, as the quality of research universities improves in many parts of the country. By and large, the fastest rates of growth in high-tech employment have been in the Southwest and Southeast, with the older manufacturing belt, despite its well-established university base, falling behind, as table 4 demonstrates.

Reagan also brought into public discussion at the highest level the question of retraining workers, believed to be offloaded permanently from the older basic industries, for jobs in the high-technology or service sectors. There is, no doubt, a legitimate public role for this kind of activity. I would observe, however, as an economic historian, that it should be a reserve role. The best training for jobs has been done by firms that needed additional labor. The factories have been, without question, the most efficient vocational schools. In a high-growth, low-unemployment economy it will pay private firms (or consortia of private firms) to finance the retraining process, perhaps with some tax incentive. This would not deny the need for some publicly financed retraining; but, to the maximum extent possible, the private sector should undertake the task.

Finally, there is a legitimate public role in helping provide infrastructure to accelerate the diffusion of new communications. It has been suggested, for example, in a recent British study that the communications revolution could be radically accelerated if consumers were provided with the basic facilities to permit exploitation of two-way communication ("tele-shopping"), financial services ("tele-banking"), and other possibilities. The costs were estimated in the range of $5–20

TABLE 4. Relative Distribution of High-Technology Jobs by Selected States, 1979 and 1975

State	Percent of U.S. High-Tech Employment, 1979	Percent of U.S. High-Tech Employment, 1975	Percent Change, 1975–1979
Western States			
Arizona	1.59	1.28	24.2
California	15.85	14.40	10.1
Colorado	1.46	1.30	12.3
Nevada	0.10	0.06	66.6
Texas	3.96	3.28	20.7
Utah	0.49	0.37	32.4
Washington	0.53	0.35	51.4
New England States			
Connecticut	2.60	2.70	−3.7
Maine	0.29	0.21	38.1
Massachusetts	6.13	5.80	5.7
New Hampshire	1.00	0.70	42.9
Rhode Island	0.53	0.55	3.6
Vermont	0.44	0.38	15.8
Mideast/Great Lake States			
Illinois	6.69	7.89	−15.2
Michigan	2.54	2.51	1.2
Minnesota	2.89	2.60	11.2
New Jersey	5.02	5.75	−12.4
New York	10.34	11.74	−11.9
Ohio	4.46	5.11	−12.7
Pennsylvania	5.79	6.75	−14.2
Southern States			
Florida	2.71	2.10	29.0
Georgia	0.78	0.65	27.7
Maryland	1.03	1.00	3.0
North Carolina	2.31	1.89	22.2
Virginia	1.11	1.23	−9.8

SOURCE: Calculated from Massachusetts Division of Employment Security, *High Technology Employment in Massachusetts and Selected States* (Boston, 1981). Reproduced in "Location of High Technology Firms and Regional Economic Development," a staff study prepared for the use of the Subcommittee on Monetary and Fiscal Policy of the Joint Economic Committee, June 1, 1982, p. 13.

billion in a country the size of the United Kingdom or the German Federal Republic. Most of the financing could be done by the private sector; but, aside from encouraging the enterprise, public policy would have to assume responsibility with respect to standards, definition of responsibilities, and links with existing telecommunications networks.

In such an enterprise, a measure of public investment would also be necessary to assure that the educational, medical, and other social potentialities of the communications system were provided. Those potentialities might well include the use of television and other modern communications systems in job retraining.

This is a matter of considerable importance. The fact is that, in education and research (including interaction among research groups and between research groups and the private sector), the potentialities of existing communications technologies far outstrip the uses to which they are now being put. The outcome is a joint product of the failure of public authorities to provide the communications infrastructure and the extraordinary sluggishness and conservatism of academic administrators and teachers. (I speak as one who began teaching in 1940.) There are, it is true, certain kinds of communication in academic life which must remain bilateral or be conducted in small, intimate groups. There is no substitute for direct, private talks between student and teacher and protracted, exploratory talks with colleagues on difficult unsolved problems. But important parts of academic life could be conducted more efficiently by means of television and other forms of communication. The possibilities of two-way communication, permitting live questions and discussions, should enrich such teaching. Similarly, new forms of communication could permit intimate, sustained two-way discussions among those conducting research in similar fields and, even, the holding of seminars among participants in different places.

Such communications could also permit easier and more regular exchanges between business firms and those doing related research in universities, a form of exchange now rapidly increasing.

C. *Rehabilitating the Older Basic Industries*

There is a quiet, serious debate going on among economists and others over whether the United States requires an industrial policy—that is, a publicly financed effort to rehabilitate the older basic industries.

On the one hand, there are those who argue that the falling behind of certain basic industries has gone so far, in a prolonged process, that the scale of investment to modernize their capital stock is beyond the capacity of firms whose cash flow has been atttenuated by the combined effects of a series of recessions and the pressure on profits of unrelenting foreign competition. Therefore, a government investment bank, like the RFC of the 1930s, should be created to provide both necessary capital and loan guarantees which, in effect, lower the rates at which firms can borrow in the capital market.

On the other hand, there are those who hold that public subsidy will waste resources by sustaining industrial structures that simply cannot survive in an environment of international competition. They argue that it is both bad economics and bad public policy to sustain such white elephants. The rigors of competitive markets should decide which firms and industries survive and which fail—for, once committed, governments will be pressed hard to throw good money after bad and, soon or late, will seek self-defeating protectionist measures to keep the firms and industries afloat. Indeed, the central thrust of the steel industry is that tariffs or other forms of substantial protection are already required and justified given the fact that foreign steel firms, government-owned or operating with government support, are using the U.S. market as a dumping ground for steel sold far below prices in foreign domestic markets.

There is a good deal of evidence in support of the skeptical view. Government subsidies of one kind or another can permit the modernization of equipment at lower cost than, say, the flotation of new issues in the private capital market; and a protected domestic market would increase the cash flow of firms at considerable cost to the consumer and to U.S. export interests in other sectors. But more than new equipment is involved in reversing the decline of an industry. Vital new management is often necessary as well as a change in workers' attitudes. The experience of the United Kingdom with government subsidies to industry is, for example, by no means uniform, but, on balance, it is not encouraging. Management was not, in all cases, adequate to lead the turnaround to competitiveness and, for whatever reasons, labor did not always join in what had to be a partnership effort if it were to succeed. The experiences of France, Germany, and Japan with industrial policies are, on balance, more hopeful.

Under clearly specified conditions, I am inclined to believe that a selective program of public assistance in the revival of basic industries may be useful. I hold that view because of the multiple forces that have brought the basic industries to their present weakened status and the complexity of the problem of an effective return to competitive status.

By way of introduction, it is worth noting that the U.S. motor vehicle industry is at the center of the story because a substantial proportion of the output of other basic industries flows as inputs to the manufacture of motor vehicles. As early as 1938, 17 percent of steel in all forms, half the output of strip and alloy steel, 90 percent of rubber manufacture, and 90 percent of gasoline production were linked to automobile manufacture. Table 5, based on an input-output table calculated by Wassily Leontief, exhibits the effect on employment of a $1 billion decline in automobile sales in 1973–1974.

As of 1978, about 21 percent of steel output of all kinds still flowed to the automobile industry; in depressed 1982, about 15 percent.

There is, of course, more to the rise and decline of the basic industries than the early glory and later vicissitudes of the U.S. motor vehicle industry (see chart 6), but the linkage is significant.

At some risk of oversimplification, the rise and decline of the American basic industries can be seen as a sequence with the following characteristics:

— An initial advantage (reaching back to the second decade of the century) arising from the precocious U.S. entrance into the age of the mass automobile, which provided a technological lead in steel, machine tools, rubber, and oil refining as well as in motor vehicle manufacture itself.

TABLE 5. Estimate of Employment Reduction Associated with a Decline of $1 Billion in U.S. Automobile Sales, 1973–1974

Industry	Employment Decline
Motor vehicle manufacturing	22,900
Other industries	
Iron and steel	4,600
Wholesale and retail trade	4,420
Fabricated metal products	4,170
Nonelectrical machinery	2,650
Textiles	1,900
Electrical machinery	1,840
Rubber	1,340
Glass	760
All other	11,360
Total, other industries	33,040
Total, all industries	55,940

SOURCE: Wassily Leontief, reported in the *New York Times*, December 8, 1974.

— This advantage led to an environment of complacency in management and a neglect of R&D. In their prime these industries generated leaders whose background and interests led to failures of understanding and communication between top management and those conducting R&D as well as underfinanced and misdirected R&D efforts. A good many inventions that emerged from U.S. R&D laboratories in basic industries first appeared as innovations abroad. The emphasis here on the quality of management and, especially, on the weak linkage of management to the potentialities of R&D in the old basic industries may appear to some to be overdrawn. But it should be recalled that the American industries which have maintained their competitive vitality all arose from laboratories and sustained strong, continuous ties to R&D—for example, electricity and electronics, chemicals, and aerospace. American agriculture, too, with its intimate ties to the land grant colleges, belongs in this category. Parallel, sustained linkages were never built up in motor vehicles, steel, and machine tools.

— The prosperity of the industries in the period (say, 1945–1970) led labor to seek and management to grant high real

CHART 6. The U.S. Motor Vehicle Industry, 1895–1982

A. Production

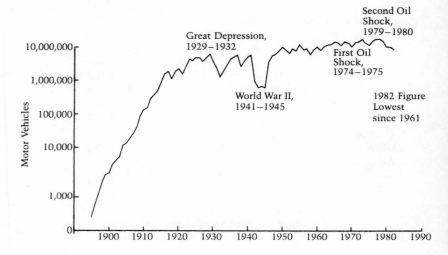

B. Rate of Growth

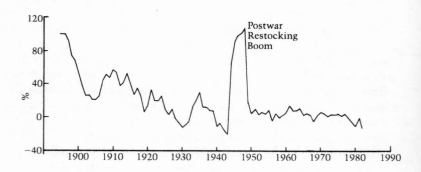

NOTE: Section B is a five-year moving average except annual figures for 1979–1982.

SOURCE: Motor Vehicles Manufacturers Association, Detroit.

wages and permitted labor leaders to concentrate on maximizing the labor share rather than the long-run viability of the industry and its employment prospects.

— When the U.S. basic industries were challenged by the arrival of the mass automobile age in Western Europe and Japan in the 1950s and 1960s, they were vulnerable. The industrial equipment in Western Europe and Japan was new; their rates of growth were much higher than in the United States, permitting large-scale plowback of profits; the leadership was more open to new ideas and on the attack rather than the defensive. U.S. automobile imports began their rapid rise in the second half of the 1960s.

— The rate of growth of the motor vehicle complex (including steel) decelerated sharply in the late 1960s and was hit doubly hard by the explosion of energy prices in 1973–1974. The rise in energy prices both reduced the real incomes of potential automobile purchasers and induced economy of use, including the purchase of smaller imported vehicles. The easing of the real price of oil in the period 1975–1978 then sent a confusing signal: a good many U.S. consumers, now skeptical of the reality of an energy crisis, turned back to larger U.S. models and the newly produced small U.S. cars did not sell well. Then came the second jump in oil prices, which convinced consumers about small cars; but their position was weakened by high interest rates, a fall in real wages, and high unemployment. With the industry in palpable danger, labor cooperated to help salvage Chrysler; but employment fell off severely in the whole group of industries linked to the fate of U.S. motor vehicle manufacture.

— Meanwhile, with investment in plant and equipment generally low after 1979, orders for steel, machine tools, and other basic industry products fell off, quite aside from reduced orders from motor vehicle manufactures.

— With profits reduced or negative and capacity utilization low, it was hard to justify or to finance large capital outlays to modernize plant.

Thus, in steel production, as of 1978, the U.S. was using 43 percent more energy per ton of steel than Japan; as of 1979, 53 percent of Japanese steel was produced by continuous casting versus 17 percent in the United States. By 1980, Japanese automobile and steel production for the first time had exceeded that of the United States.

This was the disheartening setting in which some analysts took the view that the day of the older basic industries had passed, and it was time to let them go and move to an information and service society.

As indicated earlier, I am skeptical that such a conclusion is justified; and I specified forces or potential forces at work which could radically alter the outlook for the basic industries.

The first condition for success in such an enterprise in revival is to get the economy moving forward on a path of sustained noninflationary growth. No one can be sure how much of the present distress of the basic industries is due to a structural loss of competitive viability and how much is due to a deep recession marked by the high interest rates. But analyses of the steel industry suggest a powerful and quite stable link between U.S. steel consumption and changes in real GNP, over the period 1960–1981 (see chart 7). The effort to control inflation by high real interest rates has borne with peculiarly heavy weight on the older basic industries.

Clearly, the gravity of the structural problem confronted in the steel and other basic industries cannot be assessed until we return to sustained high-growth rates. Or, put another way, if we do not return to sustained high growth, no industrial policy in the United States is likely to be effective. Moreover, a sustained U.S. noninflationary boom would lead the world economy back to sustained growth and reduce the pressures for dumping by foreign manufacturers on the U.S. market.

The second condition for a revival of the basic industries is the emergence of leaders who are capable of understanding the implication of the new technological possibilities and who are comfortable with the process of innovation. One aspect of the latter quality is an ability to foster a sense of authentic partnership in the effort of modernization with the labor force and union leadership.

The third condition is that there be a serious answering response from the union leadership of the kind exhibited by Douglas Fraser when Chrysler was in extremis.

If these three conditions were satisfied—a setting of sustained expansion, vigorous innovational entrepreneurship, and

CHART 7. Calculated Relationship between Steel Consumption and GNP, 1960–1981

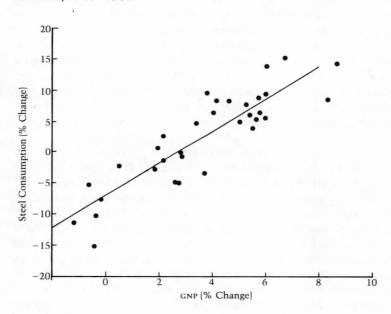

Average Behavior

Percent Change in GNP ($ 1972)	Percent Change in Steel Consumption
−2.3	−12.9
−1.3	−10.3
−0.3	−7.7
0.7	−5.1
1.7	−2.6
2.7	0.0
3.7	2.6
4.7	5.2
5.7	7.8

SOURCE: Elizabeth Bossong, manager, Economic Research, United States Steel Corporation.

labor cooperation—it might prove to be the case that private capital markets would be willing to take the risks of financing the massive reequipment that the basic industries evidently require. But the estimated orders of magnitude are large; and it is wholly possible that loans or loan guarantees by some new version of the RFC might be necessary and, in the end, highly profitable to the society. To avoid the emergence of white elephants requiring one form or another of corrosive, protracted public subsidy, the administrator of a new RFC would have to be as hardheaded and demanding as Jesse Jones was a half-century earlier.

I would greatly prefer explicit subsidy to that other form of subsidy we call protectionism. The battle to assure that GATT rules are honored is legitimate and should be conducted with vigor and a sense of legitimacy. There is an element of truth in the proposition that most other governments in the advanced industrial world press their industrial interests harder than does the United States. But there is a great deal more to the problems of the basic industries than "unfair foreign competition." Tariffs or other forms of protectionism would offer no guarantee that industry and labor in the basic industries would undertake the measures required for a reversal of their recent decline, and a U.S. adoption of protectionism in the basic industries might be a decisive blow to the hard-pressed liberal world trading system which is one of the major achievements of the post-1945 world.

D. *Coping with the Fifth Kondratieff Upswing*

The analysis in chapter 5 suggests that policy toward investment in food and raw materials (including the control of environmental degradation) is, on balance, likely to remain a major feature of the 1980s and beyond. But, evidently, as of 1983 the softening of energy prices is an urgent matter and is an appropriate place to begin (see chart 8). As we are all acutely aware, the gyrations of oil prices since 1973 have been a powerful, but not exclusive, force in determining the fluctuations and trends in the world economy. The sharp recessions of 1974–1975 and 1979–1980 were clearly related to the two oil price increases. The recession of 1981–1982 was not: it was the

CHART 8. The Real Oil Price: Two Versions

A. Current and Real U.S. Crude Oil Prices, 1962–1982 ($ 1981)

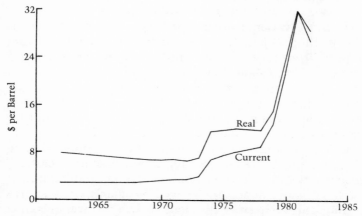

NOTE: U.S. oil price controls damped the increase in domestic prices down to decontrol in 1981, relative to the course of international oil prices.
SOURCE: *United States Petroleum Statistics 1982 (Preliminary).*

B. Purchasing Power of a Barrel of OPEC Oil in the Industrial Countries, 1973–1982

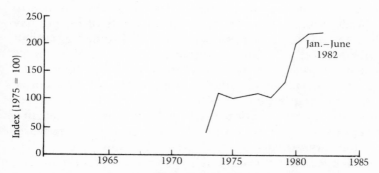

NOTE: Oil Export Price Index/Industrial Countries Export Price Index.
SOURCE: IMF International Financial Statistics.

product of a purposeful monetarist effort to wring inflation out of the American economic system, conducted against a background of falling real (and, for a time, absolute) oil prices and declining agricultural prices.

The two upward convulsions in oil prices set in motion efforts in conservation, substitution for oil, and increased non-OPEC oil drilling which altered the structure of energy demand and supply. This process reduced the role of OPEC in the world energy market from about 65 percent of non-Communist world oil consumption to about 40 percent. The stagnation of the world economy in the period 1979–1982, against this background, yielded an unprecedented absolute decline in world energy consumption. This did not occur in 1974–1975.

There is an irony here which should, parenthetically, be noted. Macroeconomics does not regard movements in particular prices as relevant to the overall course of production and prices. Such movements are viewed as changes in relative prices. But, obviously, since the close of 1972 the overall course of the world economy has been substantially shaped by the erratic interaction between energy prices and the macroperformance of particular economies. In fact, the short-run political fate of the nominally monetarist Reagan administration will be greatly affected by the course of real oil prices in 1983–1984.

To maintain minimum control over world prices in the face of the circumstances of 1979–1983, OPEC was forced to cut production from about 31 million barrels of oil per day (mbod) in 1979 to 18 in 1982. Saudi Arabia absorbed about half of this decline, reducing its output from a peak of about 10 mbod (perhaps higher) to 4 (perhaps lower). In March 1983 OPEC, after protracted negotiation, appeared to agree on a price cut and the distribution of the burden of a further reduction of about 1 mbod in production, estimated as required to prevent a further decline in world oil prices at the bottom of the world recession. As noted earlier, it was uncertain whether this agreement would recapture stability in the world oil market.

Whether OPEC would maintain discipline in the face of its fragile agreement of March 1983 or be caught up in a competitive price war for market shares was a matter for speculation. But the short-run prospects for the world oil price were probably for either stability or some further decline.

In the latter case, the general effects of such a development were evident enough. They would simply reverse, in a milder form, the impact of the two oil price jumps of the 1970s.

For oil importers, there would be a rise in real income, a stimulus to consumption expenditures, a general dampening effect on the inflation rate. Within the United States, energy-exporting regions would be adversely affected; but that process would also reduce revenues from the so-called windfall profits tax and thereby tend to enlarge the federal deficit. The oil price decline of 1980–1982 caused a sharp reduction in marginal oil drilling as well as a shelving of plans for synthetic plants. Energy-related investment, which had become a high proportion of total nonresidential housing investment by 1981, was already declining in 1982–1983. The number of oil and gas drilling rigs at work, 4,160 in February 1982, was 2,192 twelve months later. A further energy price decline would exacerbate this trend. There might also be, as in 1976–1979, a tendency for consumers to purchase larger automobiles as gasoline prices eased, a phenomenon detectable in the last quarter of 1982 and early in 1983.

In the developing world, oil importers would experience an easing in their balance of payments positions (for example, Brazil and India); oil exporters (for example, Mexico, Venezuela, Indonesia, and Nigeria) would face further difficulties requiring, quite possibly, concerted international financial support.

If we could be confident that the downturn in the world oil price signaled the beginning of a protracted phase of cheap energy in the world economy—or, even, of constant energy prices—the turn of events could be wholeheartedly welcomed. Despite the vicissitudes of energy-producing countries and regions, cheaper energy is better for the world economy than expensive energy.

The problem is that no one can confidently project the effects of a revival of the world economy from its three years of virtual stagnation on the demand for energy in general and oil in particular. Two questions are embedded in this problem. How strong and pervasive will the expansion be? How has the demand for energy (and oil) been structurally transformed by the erratic rise in the real price of energy since 1973? Put another way, by how much has the overall energy (and oil) content of a unit of real GNP been permanently lowered in the various nations and regions of the world economy, and will that decline level off or proceed on a downward path? Clearly, a good deal of both energy conservation and diversification to nonoil sources of energy has occurred; but no one knows how much or whether it will result in a progressive decline or constitute a once-over change which will yield a renewed rise in energy consumption when economies resume expansion.

In a lucid effort to grapple with this complex problem, my colleague Michael Kennedy has made the following calculations. He first breaks out the components in the dramatic decline of OPEC production between 1979 and 1982 as follows:

OPEC's Short-Run Problem (mbod)

Output in 1979	31.5
Decrease in world demand	7.5
Increase in world supply (mainly Mexico and U.K.)	2.0
Inventory swing	4.0
Output in 1982	18.0

Kennedy assumes that half the decline in world oil demand was due to conservation, induced by high oil prices, half due to the recession.

Looking to the future, he assumes as a base case no disruption in OPEC oil supply; average 3 percent real growth in the world economy; an effective OPEC oil production limit of 27 mbod; and a price elasticity of demand of −0.6 percent. The latter means that a 1 percent rise in the real oil price results in a decline of 0.6 percent in the amount purchased.

In the next few years, Kennedy assumes two factors will operate to increase the world demand for oil—namely, a reversal of the sharp run-down of inventories in recent years and recovery in the world economy. On the other hand, he assumes large (9 mbod) excess capacity in OPEC; and this surplus overhanging the market prevents a price increase down to, say, 1985. From that time on, an annual rate of increase in the real price of oil of 4.5 percent unfolds down to the year 2005. If effective OPEC production capacity is assumed to be 23 mbod (rather than 27), the price rise begins promptly with world recovery; if taken at 31 mbod, the price increase comes later

CHART 9. Lead Times in Domestic Energy Development

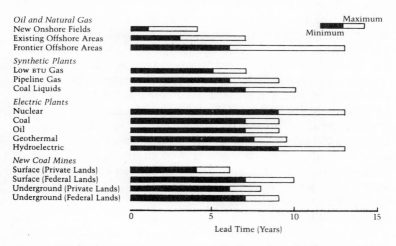

SOURCE: Modified from National Academy of Engineering (1973) and U.S. Geological Survey (1975).

(1990). In alternative scenarios, the course of the real oil price in an econometric exercise of this kind also proves sensitive to assumptions about the rate of real growth in the world economy and the price elasticity of demand for oil. But under all scenarios, there is a long-run rise in the real price of oil.

Such speculative calculations would be of merely academic interest if the production of energy was promptly responsive to market prices and expected short-run profits. We could stand back and watch unfolding events give us the answer.

There are two reasons why this cheerful acceptance of the short-run market outcome is unsatisfactory. First, important types of energy investment take rather long periods of time. Chart 9 exhibits calculations of lead times for various kinds of energy investment. Energy R&D evidently has even longer lead times, and the reduction of such outlays by the Reagan administration may prove quite costly.

Second, standing back from the sequence of fluctuations

in the real price of oil, it is clear that the trend in that price (and energy prices in general) has been upward since 1973 (see chart 7). There are, in my view, good reasons to believe that the basic analysis of energy experts over the past decade has been correct—namely, that the world economy faces a historical transition of uncertain length away from oil to other energy sources and probably a resumption of a rise in the real price of oil. New finds have been and, no doubt, will continue to be made; and the extremely intensive drilling after the second oil price increase in areas with known reserves halted, for a time, the decline in U.S. oil production. But the prospect remains that, under normal growth in the world economy, the real price of energy would, in time, continue to increase and the diversification of the world's energy base toward coal, nuclear power, and other energy sources be required.

It would be difficult to construct a less rational or satisfactory way of adjusting the world economy to the realities of the energy situation and prospects than that which history provided in the decade 1973–1983: two convulsive price increases, the second clearly excessive, followed by two periods of decline in the real oil price. The periods of oil price remission were caused in good part by the recessions imposed by the price increases. The world economy responded to each short-run movement like a cork in the sea. Both producers and consumers acted as if current market trends would persist. This yielded, in each phase, exaggerated responses, including, in some cases, long-term commitments that had to be painfully reversed.

Rational long-run policies are rarely achieved in a complex world economy, notably in a field where the policies of sovereign governments play so large a role. Nevertheless, the world community should strive to do better over the next decade than it did in the painful decade behind us.

One might well respond that the ideal solution would be for OPEC to break up and let competitive market forces take over as, say, in the world's grain markets. Putting aside the real elements of government intervention in the relatively competitive grain markets, the problem with respect to oil is its marked difference from most other commodities. Large additions to productive capacity are created in a rather odd way. A great deal of high-cost drilling is required to establish major new fields. As noted earlier, it is an extraordinary fact that 90 percent of the world's oil production is derived from 5 percent of its oil fields. Once established, the marginal cost of lifting oil from them is low; and the risks in further drilling, to develop fully the potential output of a known field, are much less than for authentic exploratory drilling. But, in all cases, the pumping of oil runs down reserves which must be supplanted if the production level is to be maintained. The upshot is that the price of oil must cover the high risk of exploratory drilling if an adequate incentive to maintain (or expand or minimize the decline in) production levels is to exist. Conventional short-period price analysis is, thus, quite inadequate. And this is why oil production has tended to fall under one form of monopolistic arrangement or another in which production was restricted to maintain, more or less wisely, the long-run viability of this peculiar industry by prices in excess of the marginal cost of pumping oil from existing fields.

Historically, the unpopular and apparently sinister process of restraining production to maintain an oil price consistent with drilling on a scale capable of replacing or enlarging reserves has been conducted, with greater or lesser wisdom, by a sequence of four monopolistic institutions: the Standard Oil Trust, when the bulk of the world's oil came from the eastern United States; the Texas Railroad Commission, when its locus shifted to Texas; the "Seven Sisters," when American, British, and Dutch firms discovered and developed oil on all the continents; and, then, OPEC.

If OPEC, which seized in 1973 the role of long-run price setter from the international oil companies, should disintegrate, a cutthroat price war is conceivable in which each oil producer would seek to maximize his market share and short-run foreign exchange revenues. It is because the consequences for all oil producers would be so disastrous that one would expect, if minimum rationality prevails within OPEC, that the producers would continue to agree on somewhat reduced production quotas and a somewhat lower price. But minimum rationality may not prevail, and we could experience a phase of radically lowered prices with temporary benign effects. The effects would be temporary because an extremely low price would simultaneously run down existing reserves and discourage investment in both oil exploration and the development of long-run alternatives to oil. After a cheap oil binge, the world economy would, depending on its rate of growth and the effects of cheap oil on energy economy, confront another energy price crisis for which its lagging energy investment had rendered it singularly ill prepared. Indeed, some analysts believe negative investment responses to the falling real price of oil in the past several years have already posed that danger for the mid or late 1980s.

What are the implications of all this for U.S. energy policy? I believe that the U.S. should pursue steadily the purposeful goal of seeking minimum dependence on oil imports, notably imports from the volatile Persian Gulf area; and it should systematically prepare for its almost certain future role as a large coal exporter and producer of synthetics from coal and shale. This means also that public policy should continue to encourage energy conservation.

Specifically, if a true oil price war breaks out, the U.S. should shield the American economy from its impact on production and conservation by an oil import tax, although the occasion might be used rapidly to fill up the nation's oil strategic reserve at low international prices. The import tax should be structured to hold the domestic oil price steady, rising with a decline in the international oil price, falling with an increase.

If OPEC holds together, the United States should act in three ways. First, it should recognize that the total effect on the U.S. economy of importing a barrel of oil differs from that of producing an equivalent amount of energy at home. There are adverse balance of payments, inflation, employment, and security factors that ought to be taken into account. The minimum difference is estimated at about 30 percent by William Hogan of Harvard. A tariff on imported oil is, therefore, justified. Second, public policy should continue to support strongly energy R&D and support the preparations for a future large-scale synthetics industry and a large coal export capability. Third, the U.S. should encourage the emergence of a global institution, embracing producers and consumers, which would seek to achieve continuity in supply and less volatile price movements than those experienced in the past decade, which have gravely damaged the interests of both producers and consumers. The task would not be easy. Since its beginning in 1960, OPEC itself has had to try to reconcile the conflicting interests of foreign exchange surplus and hard-pressed developing countries—a tension now complicated by intense political conflicts. On the producers' side, the non-OPEC exporters would have to find ways to work with OPEC. And then common ground would have to be found among the importers and between exporters and importers. Nevertheless, such arrangements have existed and, at times, done useful work with respect to coffee, tin, and, before the Second World War, timber. The U.S.S.R. participated in the latter consultative group. The objective would be to make gradual, incremental price adjustments in the light of both short-term market circumstances and the legitimate long-run interests of both producers and consumers.

The actual price outcome over a period of time would depend on these four factors:
— The rate of growth experienced in the world economy.
— What new oil discoveries prove to be.
— The policies toward their reserves of oil producers.
— The degree of seriousness of oil importers with respect to their investments in the production of all forms of energy and in energy conservation.

Energy is by no means the only area which requires enlarged investment to provide a satisfactory resource base for the American economy. For example, the declining Ogallala water basin, running from the Texas Panhandle to Nebraska, poses a major problem for the nation as well as the region. The maintenance of high agricultural productivity will require some combination of water economy, increased efficiency in dry farming, and, if feasible, water transfers. And there is a range of other water problems in other regions, some of which fall under the rubric of infrastructure, discussed in section E, below. There are also problems of maintaining the forests for the long pull as a source of timber and areas of recreation and of providing a flow of investment to sustain an environment of clean air and water. In different degree all these resource problems involve issues of public policy.

The most urgent resource problems requiring a change in

public policy, however, lie in Latin America, Africa, the Middle East, and Asia and in the relations between those southern regions and the industrial North.

Chapter 5 outlined the case for regarding their problems of energy, food, raw materials, and the control of environmental degradation as key to the creation of a long-run North-South partnership effort. I presented this proposition as flowing naturally from my view of the world economy as still caught up in the Fifth Kondratieff Upswing, despite the current softening of energy, agricultural, and industrial raw material prices. Chapter 5 also cited estimates of the very large investments required to provide those regions with a resource base capable of sustaining the high rates of growth which are normal and required, given their intermediate stage of development and generally high rates of population increase. Finally, their rising importance as export markets for the U.S., Western Europe, and Japan was underlined.

I might note, parenthetically, that the concept that a North-South partnership should be built on the basis of an authentic common interest in this array of resource problems has been widely perceived without the benefit of an economic historian's conclusion that we are experiencing the Fifth Kondratieff Upswing. The report of the Brandt Commission, *North-South*, devoted several chapters to this theme, although these elements in the report were overwhelmed in its public impact by an overriding plea for a massive transfer of resources from North to South on the dubious grounds that the North lacked adequate investment opportunities to achieve full employment. The report of the Herrera Commission, appointed by the secretary-general of the Organization of American States (OAS) to define areas for economic cooperation in the Western Hemisphere, isolated agriculture, energy, raw materials, and certain environmental problems among its seven priority tasks. The Association of Southeast Asian Nations (ASEAN) has defined energy and agriculture as the two top-priority areas for joint action. Indeed, at Cancún, in a little-noted intervention, President Reagan showed an awareness of the need to move in this direction. Among the five principles he set out to guide North-South economic relations, he included the following as his third point: "Guiding our assistance towards the development of self-sustaining productive activities, particularly in food and energy." Unfortunately, neither his colleagues at Cancún nor his own administration has pursued this insight seriously and systematically.

These problems are, in fact, endemic and not confined to the non-Communist world. Any analysis of the problems and prospects for the Soviet Union and the People's Republic of China over the next generation would have to include energy and agriculture high on the list of priority tasks. (A recent visitor to Austin from the P.R.C. and I chuckled when, having surveyed the major economic problems confronted by his country over the next generation, we found the list almost identical to that generated by the Texas Commission on the Year 2000: energy, water, agricultural productivity, transport, and a radical enlargement in R&D capacity.)

A sustained North-South effort to come to grips with this array of resource-related problems should, in my view, have the following essential characteristics:

1. The enterprise should be conducted primarily on a regional basis. The ultimate task is to examine sectoral investment requirements, looking a decade or more ahead and isolating projects to be financed domestically or with foreign private or official resources. This kind of technical activity does not lend itself to global gatherings, which now involve anywhere up to 150 governmental representatives.

2. The regional groups might center, in the Western Hemisphere, around the OAS and the Inter-American Development Bank (IDB); in Africa, around the African Development Bank (ADB) and the Economic Commission for Africa (ECA); in the Pacific Basin, around the Asian Development Bank (ADB). The World Bank would participate in all the regional enterprises as well as relevant global organizations, for example, the Food and Agriculture Organization (FAO). The U.S., Western Europe, and Japan would also participate in the three regional ventures, although their degree of involvement might vary with their respective regional interests. India and China might well prefer, because of their size, to deal with this array of problems via the World Bank (and the kind of consortium arrangements the World Bank has managed) rather than in multilateral committees.

3. The participants would, evidently, have to consist primarily of officials who bear serious responsibility domestically for policy toward the sectors under examination.

Where appropriate, governments may wish to engage persons from their private sectors in the process.

The setting in motion of a concerted North-South effort to enlarge investment, domestic and foreign, in these resource-related fields obviously does not constitute a complete economic policy relating the advanced industrial to the developing countries. The overriding responsibility of the North to the South (as well as to the citizens of the North) is to regain a high regular growth rate with inflation under reliable control. Without this condition, the debt rollovers of 1982–1983 are likely to buy only a little time before new, dangerous financial crises again emerge. If that condition is satisfied, the foreign exchange earning capacity of the developing countries will increase, their debt burdens will become manageable, and protectionist pressures will subside.

In addition, there is the common task of diffusing the potentialities of the Fourth Industrial Revolution to the developing regions. A good many of the new technologies are already relevant to their economies, and more will become so.

There is also a series of problems faced by some of the smaller countries in the world—notably, in Africa, the Caribbean, and Central America—where foreign aid subsidies are required if they are not to continue to retrogress with grave human, social, political, and, quite possibly, strategic consequences. The problems of these smaller countries are not all alike. In some, the problems are starkly Malthusian—that is, acute pressure of population increase against agricultural sectors of low productivity. In others, high oil import prices and low growth in the advanced industrial countries have cut their foreign exchange availabilities and thus their capacity to sustain themselves. They generally lack the resilience to make effective adjustments to their straitened circumstances. I believe that, for converging reasons of morality and self-interest, the world community must accept responsibility in such cases; and the fact is that, despite domestic vicissitudes, the advanced industrial countries and the multilateral institutions have recognized this array of welfare problems and done a good deal to ameliorate them. Meanwhile, as time is bought, longer-term solutions should be sought which, notably in Africa, the Caribbean, and Central America, are likely to take the form of more effective subregional economic associations.

But, as the developing countries confront a generation of maximum pressure of population increase on food and other resources, a time when a good many of them have come to the stage when they are also capable of a rapid absorption of technologies and rapid growth, a North-South partnership centered on the critical resource sectors appears the natural centerpiece in a relationship of growing mutual interdependence.

E. *Rebuilding the Nation's Infrastructure*

Although a consciousness that we have been running down the nation's infrastructure and living off capital has been growing, the scale and character of the problem justify the following extended quotation from *America in Ruins*, by Pat Choate and Susan Walter, as well as a close examination of chart 10 and the statistics in table 6:

> Despite a number of recent analyses, the precise condition of the nation's public works inventory—and the future investments we face—remains unknown. While comprehensive and reliable information is still lacking, the partial information that is available paints a disturbing picture:
>
> The nation's 42,500-mile Interstate Highway System, only now approaching completion, is deteriorating at a rate requiring reconstruction of 2,000 miles of road per year. Because adequate funding for rehabilitation and reconstruction was not forthcoming in the late 1970s, over 8,000 miles of this system and 13 percent of its bridges are now beyond their designed service life and must be rebuilt. Although the system constitutes less than one percent of the nation's highways, it handles over 20 percent of all highway traffic. Its further decline will adversely affect the national economy and the well-being of thousands of communities and individual firms.
>
> The costs of rehabilitation and new construction nec-

essary to maintain existing levels of service on non-urban highways will exceed $700 billion during the 1980s. Even excluding the estimated $75 billion required to complete the unconstructed final 1,500 miles of the Interstate System, the balance required for rehabilitation and reconstruction is still greater than *all* the public works investments made by *all* units of government in the 1970s. Since inflation in highway construction has averaged 12.5 percent since 1973 (doubling costs each six years), continuation of present investment levels will permit less than one-third of needs to be met in this decade.

One of every five bridges in the United States requires either major rehabilitation or reconstruction. The Department of Transportation has estimated the costs of this task to be as high as $33 billion. Yet in Fiscal Year 1981 Federal Highway Authorizations, only $1.3 billion was allocated to repair bridge deficiencies.

Estimates of the amounts required to rebuild the deteriorating road beds and rolling stock of the railroads of the Northeast and Midwest are not available. While economic necessity may compel reductions in CONRAIL trackage by as much as half, or total reorganization of the system itself, this will not obviate the need for rail modernization. Railroads will play a critical role in national efforts to reduce transportation energy consumption and ship more coal to power plants to replace imported oil. This is a national issue of major importance. A viable eastern rail system is essential to the economic health of the western and southern systems since these regional rail systems can thrive only as part of a national network linking all markets and centers of production.

No reliable estimates exist of the investments required to modernize our ports, but numerous instances exist of harbor facilities unable to service efficiently world shipping coming to American docks. Vessels in some ports must wait for as long as a month to pick up their cargo.

The nation's municipal water supply needs will make heavy demands upon capital markets in the 1980s. The

CHART 10. Construction Spending as Percent of Total State and Local Purchases, 1955–1982

SOURCE: Elizabeth Bossong, manager, Economic Research, United States Steel Corporation.

756 urban areas with populations of over 50,000 will require between $75 billion and $110 billion to maintain their urban water systems over the next 20 years. Approximately one-fifth of these communities will face investment shortfalls, even if present water rates are doubled to produce capital for new investment. At least an additional $10–$13 billion beyond that generated by existing user charges will be required.

Over $25 billion in government funds will be required during the next five years to meet existing water pollution control standards.

Over $40 billion must be invested in New York City alone over the next nine years to repair, service and rebuild basic public works facilities that include: 1,000 bridges, two aqueducts, one large water tunnel, several reservoirs, 6,200 miles of paved streets, 6,000 miles of sewers, 6,000 miles of water lines, 6,700 subway cars, 4,500 buses, 25,000 acres of parks, 17 hospitals, 19 city university campuses, 950 schools, 200 libraries, and hundreds of fire houses and police stations. Because of its fiscal condition, New York City will be able to invest only $1.4 billion per year to repair, service, and rebuild these facilities.

At least $1 billion will be required to rebuild Cleveland's basic public works—$250 to $500 million is needed to replace and renovate the publicly-owned water system; over $150 million is required for major repairs of city bridges; and over $340 million must be spent for flood control facilities. In addition to these expenditures, Cleveland must find additional funds to rebuild or resurface 30 percent of its streets, now in a state of advanced deterioration, and to reconstruct the city's sewer collection system, which frequently floods commercial and residential buildings.

Even fiscally healthy cities face large public works investment requirements. For example, Dallas must raise almost $700 million for investment in water and sewerage treatment systems in the next nine years. More than $109 million must be generated to repair deteriorating city streets.

Over one-half of the nation's 3,500 jails are over 30 years old. At least 1,300 and perhaps as many as 3,000 of these facilities must be either totally rebuilt or substantially rehabilitated in the 1980s. This construction, in most cases, is court ordered. Thus, it often takes legal precedence over most, if not all, other public capital expenditures.

Rural facility needs, as yet unknown, are the subject of a major survey by the U.S. Department of Agriculture currently underway.

Water resource development will require major investments in *all* regions of the nation in the 1980s. The agricultural base in the old "Dustbowl" will be in jeopardy toward the end of the decade unless new water sources can be developed. After the Second World War, vast underground water resources close to the surface were tapped for irrigation. Today, this area in the Texas and Oklahoma panhandles and surrounding states has

TABLE 6. Total (Residential and Nonresidential) Public Works Investment, Gross and Net, and Depreciation, 1957–1977 (in Millions of Constant 1972 Dollars)

Year	Federal				State and Local				Total Government			
	Gross Investment	Depreciation	Depreciation as Percent of Gross Investment	Net Investment	Gross Investment	Depreciation	Depreciation as Percent of Gross Investment	Net Investment	Gross Investment	Depreciation	Depreciation as Percent of Gross Investment	Net Investment
1957	3,571	5,395	151.1	−1,824	20,374	8,325	40.86	12,049	23,945	13,720	57.30	10,225
1958	4,364	5,039	115.5	−675	21,663	8,752	40.40	12,911	26,027	13,791	52.99	12,236
1959	3,783	4,679	123.7	−896	22,081	9,128	41.34	12,953	25,864	13,807	53.38	12,057
1960	3,787	4,335	114.5	−548	22,300	9,523	42.70	12,777	26,087	13,858	53.12	12,229
1961	4,424	4,058	91.7	366	23,988	9,929	41.39	14,059	28,412	13,987	49.23	14,425
1962	4,981	3,865	77.6	1,116	24,660	10,342	41.94	14,318	29,641	14,207	47.93	15,434
1963	5,784	3,963	68.5	1,821	26,799	10,780	40.23	16,019	32,583	14,743	45.25	17,840
1964	6,602	3,756	56.9	2,846	28,652	11,259	39.30	17,393	35,254	15,015	42.59	20,239
1965	6,872	3,829	55.7	3,043	30,281	11,775	38.89	18,506	37,153	15,604	42.00	21,549
1966	7,040	3,949	56.1	3,091	32,422	12,327	38.02	20,095	39,462	16,276	41.24	23,186
1967	5,911	4,056	68.6	1,855	35,041	12,933	36.91	22,108	40,952	16,989	41.49	23,963
1968	4,401	4,132	93.9	269	36,944	13,608	36.83	23,336	41,345	17,740	42.91	23,605
1969	3,684	4,170	113.2	−486	34,749	14,277	41.09	20,472	38,433	18,447	48.00	19,986
1970	3,716	4,189	112.7	−473	32,741	14,902	45.51	17,839	36,457	19,091	52.37	17,376
1971	3,931	4,185	106.5	−254	31,882	15,510	48.65	16,372	35,813	19,695	54.99	15,538
1972	4,010	4,164	103.8	−154	31,125	16,111	51.76	15,014	35,135	20,275	57.71	14,860
1973	4,128	4,138	100.2	−10	31,135	16,712	53.68	14,423	35,263	20,850	59.13	14,413
1974	3,845	4,094	106.5	−249	32,147	17,335	53.92	14,812	35,992	21,429	59.54	14,563
1975	3,482	4,026	115.6	−544	30,680	17,997	58.66	12,683	34,162	22,023	64.47	12,139
1976	3,765	3,954	105.0	−189	27,510	18,571	67.51	8,939	31,275	22,525	72.02	8,750
1977	4,122	3,893	94.4	229	25,826	19,076	73.86	6,750	30,037	22,969	76.47	7,068

SOURCE: J. C. Musgrave, BEA, special tabulation; United States Department of Commerce, A Study of Public Works Investment in the United States (Washington, D.C., 1980), p. I-63.

over 10 million acres under irrigation (23 percent of the nation's total irrigated farmland). This irrigated production produces over 40 percent of the nation's processed beef and major portions of wheat, sorghums, and other crops that supply much of America's agricultural exports. The region's water source is being depleted. At present rates it will be gone by the year 2000. The reversion of the region's agricultural production back to low-yield dryland farming would have a devastating effect on the economics of six states. It would seriously harm the nation's balance of payments and ultimately reduce the value of the dollar in international markets. If this production is to be retained, major public works to bring surplus water from adjacent regions are required.

Even such water "surplus" areas as New England, Pennsylvania, New Jersey, and New York are in water crises, in part, because of the inadequacies of their water supply, storage, treatment, and distribution systems that become apparent in time of drought.

A large number of the nation's 43,500 dams require investment to reduce hazardous deficiencies. The Corps of Engineers has already inspected 9,000 of these facilities and found many of them in need of safety improvements. The funds to inspect even the balance of these dams have not been available. A majority of the dams that are potentially hazardous are privately owned and the dam owners lack the financial resources, willingness, or understanding to take remedial measures. Nor do the states have the legislative authority, funds, or trained personnel to conduct their own inspection and remedial efforts.

These are not isolated or extreme examples. They represent broad trends of decline in both the quantity and quality of virtually every type of public works facilities in the nation. Unless these trends are reversed—and soon— the number of public facilities in usable condition will fall to even more dangerous levels. (Pat Choate and Susan Walter, *America in Ruins: Beyond the Public Works Pork Barrel* [Washington, D.C.: Council of State Planning Agencies, 1981], pp. 1–5)

No authority of whom I am aware would challenge the broad implications of this account of the disintegration of the physical foundations of our society.

I noted earlier that estimates of the total investment outlays to rehabilitate and maintain the nation's physical infrastructure over the next decade or fifteen years range from about $650 to $2,500 billion. Perhaps a more useful way to grasp the order of magnitude of the problem is this: in 1965 4.1 percent of GNP was invested in public works; in 1977, 2.3 percent. An extra 2 percent of GNP would thus have to be allocated annually to public works to reattain the 1965 level, when there was substantial net investment over and above depreciation in physical infrastructures.

Two simple things can be said about this investment requirement—clearly enormous but not yet firmly measurable. It is most unlikely to be met unless a sustained noninflationary economic revival occurs which lifts public revenues and narrows greatly the federal deficit; if met, it would set up a requirement for labor in the construction industry and those supplying inputs to that industry that is likely to lift the specter of chronic technological unemployment and increase substantially the demand for steel and some other products of the older basic industries. Clearly, infrastructure investment (along with the diffusion of the new technologies, the rehabilitation of the old basic industries, and enlarged investments, at home and abroad, in resource sectors) should be one of the sectoral pillars of the boom of the 1980s and 1990s. As I trust the analysis incorporated in this book demonstrates, that boom should be rooted in enlarged investment, public and private; and, almost certainly, it will require a higher proportion of GNP invested.

Under those circumstances a good deal of thought ought to be given to how the capital for the enterprise should be raised, priorities set, wastage avoided, infrastructure investments timed to the rhythm of business fluctuations, organization at federal, state, and local levels simplified and, to the degree feasible, coordinated. This is not an occasion to summarize and pass judgment on the considerable literature bearing on these matters.

There is reasonably general agreement, however, on a few key points:

— Serious efforts to reduce graft, corruption, and wasteful delays in granting and executing public works contracts should be undertaken. Some models of good practice have emerged.

— User (or fee-for-service) charges have potentialities for expanded application and contribute to conservation and reduced waste, notably with respect to water. But, in general, after recent vicissitudes the American public is probably more ready than in the past to regard public services as requiring payment rather than as an occasion for a free ride. User charges also improve access to capital markets, guaranteeing, as they do, a flow of revenues.

— Prompt action to reduce the backlog of some $100 billion in public works projects for which federal funds have been appropriated but not used.

— And, more controversial, the creation of a federal capital budget which would permit a gearing of infrastructure outlays to other dimensions of national economic policy as well as the setting of standards for infrastructure investment which might reduce the pork barrel element that has traditionally entered decisions on public works.

The Supply-Side Economics We Need

These five major areas where new policies are required constitute supply-side economics in a quite different sense than that phrase has been used in recent years. We require more than a general undifferentiated expansion of investment in the private sector. The state of the American economy and the world economy requires expanded investment in certain particular directions: to support an energy policy at home to assure, on balance, the nation's independence of foreign energy sources; to insulate the nation to the extent possible from other sources of raw materials-push inflation; to supplement the natural vitality of the private sector in unfolding and diffusing the potentialities of the Fourth Industrial Revolution; to assure the viability of basic industries; to assure the continued momentum of the developing regions (and our exports to them) by helping them provide the resource underpinnings for their continued growth; to rebuild and maintain the nation's now eroding physical infrastructure. This kind of sustained supply-side effort appears well within our capabilities; it would surely provide ample opportunities of employment for our working force; and, except for investment in physical infrastructure, it could mainly, but not exclusively, be carried forward by the private sector if an environment of low real interest rates and confidence that inflation was under control were established.

These judgments on the technical characteristics of the tasks ahead bring us, finally, into a terrain beyond conventional economics.

7. A Conclusion

One large conclusion emerges from this effort to define a civilized synthesis to supersede the explicable but barbaric counterrevolution of 1979–1983. The tasks of the 1980s and beyond require a heightened sense of community and public action based upon it when compared with the tasks of the 1950s and 1960s. Then, with all of us lifted by the tide of favorable terms of trade and enjoying automatically rising private real incomes, we could argue about how our good fortune should be distributed. Now we must together rebuild the foundations of our economy—and the world economy—while generating and absorbing a set of new technologies.

The resource-related and infrastructure problems discussed in chapters 5 and 6 are, in different degree, inevitably within the orbit of the public sector—federal, state, and local. This is true of certain aspects of the energy problem, although an environment of deregulated gas as well as oil and coal prices is essential for the private sector to maximize energy conservation and production and to yield an efficient use of alternative fuels. It is true of water, transport, and environmental problems as well as critical dimensions of R&D. New cooperative links are required between the public sector, the private sector, and the universities in dealing with these problems as well as in assuring that the United States is in the forefront of the Fourth Industrial Revolution now under way. And, surely, the rehabilitation of the older basic industries will require an authentic partnership between labor and management if it is to be achieved and, almost certainly, will also require some elements of public support.

Above all, the heart of the problem of controlling inflation, on which depends success in all the other tasks, turns out to be a coming together of business, labor, and government, in a new institutional framework, to assure that money wage increases and the rate of increase in productivity are firmly linked. Every serious examination of this difficult problem concludes that, in the end, a satisfactory outcome can be reached only if a sense of communal purpose transcending special interests, but consonant with them, is achieved.

Looking back over the more than two centuries of national life, it is easy to conclude that this great continental society is incapable of such communal concert and that free, competitive economic markets and the raucous competitive struggle of narrow, vested interests in the political markets, at federal, state, and local levels, are the best we can do. This is, I suspect, the implicit assumption about the character of our society underlying the counter-revolution which has brought us to where we are and to the corrosive proposition that inflation can be controlled only by maintaining high levels of unemployment.

This assessment is based, I believe, on an incomplete view of our history and the nature of American society. The initial tense struggle between the Hamiltonians and Jeffersonians was resolved, in both its domestic and foreign policy dimensions, by an authentic consensus which emerged after the election of 1800. Jefferson was, in many ways, a Federalist president. Americans talked of private enterprise but from the Cumberland Road, the Erie Canal, the land grants to both railroads and the new technical colleges down to Herbert Hoover's RFC, we brought the public and private sectors together when we needed to do so. Whether in reconstructing the centers of our cities or putting men on the moon and bringing them back, in buying time for New York City or salvaging Chrysler or seeking to keep the social security system viable, we have been more of a partnership society than our textbooks in economics and government—or our conventional political rhetoric—acknowledge. A close look at the healing dynamics of our towns and cities, large and small, demonstrates that a sense of community is still alive in the land; and one can occasionally perceive it in Washington.

For in national politics, too, there have been successors to the Jeffersonian consensus. Eisenhower's passive acceptance of the New Deal and, in the end, I predict, the survival under Reagan of most of the Great Society suggest that we have known how to weave together and find appropriate balances, after contentious debate, between the public and private sectors. Even on the deepest and most intractable of all the problems we faced—the problem of race—after a bloody civil war, we have slowly made some progress toward the ideal of equality of opportunity to which we committed ourselves in the eighteenth century and which we cannot deny without ceasing to be Americans.

In traveling our country in recent years, I sense a strong, untapped will to come together to solve problems now patently out of control, a mood not unlike the one John Kennedy captured in 1960 with his campaign slogan: "Let's get this country moving again." This sense of community—of communal commitment and communal purpose—which frames and tempers and enriches our free competitive institutions is the strand in our history and culture we shall have to nurture and on which we shall have to build to transit successfully the generation ahead.

It is, I believe, the central mission of the presidential election campaign of 1984 to yield, out of its dialectic, a national consensus on this proposition and a president who will build systematically upon it.